VISUAL QUICKSTART GUIDE

Claris
Home Page 3

FOR WINDOWS AND MACINTOSH

Richard Fenno

 Peachpit Press

Visual QuickStart Guide
Claris Home Page 3
Richard Fenno

Peachpit Press
1249 Eighth Street
Berkeley, CA 94710
(510) 524-2178
(510) 524-2221 (fax)

Find us on the World Wide Web at: http://www.peachpit.com

Peachpit Press is a division of Addison Wesley Longman

Editors: Adam Ray, Jeni Englander
Project Editor: Marjorie Baer
Production Coordinator: Kate Reber
Copy Editors: Gail Nelson, Terry O'Donnell, Elissa Rabellino
Indexer: Nancy Kopper
Cover design: The Visual Group
Production: Jeni Englander

Notice of liability
The information in this book is distributed on an "As is" basis, without warranty. While every precaution has been taken in the preparation of this book, neither the author nor Peachpit Press shall have any liability to any person or entity with respect to any loss or damage caused or alleged to be caused directly or indirectly by the instructions contained in this book or by the computer software and hardware products described herein.

ISBN: 0-201-69647-9

0 9 8 7 6 5 4 3 2 1

Printed and bound in the United States of America

♻ Printed on recycled paper

To Jan Gillespie—my mate
and
Brendan Fenno and Caitlin Fenno—my children

Special thanks to:

Nancy Davis at Peachpit Press and Adam Ray and crew at Big Tent and Dave Dumas at FileMaker, Inc.

Marjorie Baer—you are truly beyond category.

My many saxophone buddies on and off the Internet, including Steve Goodson at saxgourmet.com (where you can check a serial number for manufacturing date), Paul Lindemeyer for *Celebrating the Saxophone* and solid criticism, Peter Fluck—better known as saxmanpete@webtv.com, for selling me my dream bass saxophone, Nick Rail at nickrailmusic.com, and all the cats and kitties over at alt.music.saxophone.

Our dog Zeke for scheduling his walks when my muse wasn't functional.

All my family and friends for tolerating and supporting me through this project.

TABLE OF CONTENTS

TABLE OF CONTENTS

INTRODUCTION

Figure 1. This is your raw HTML.

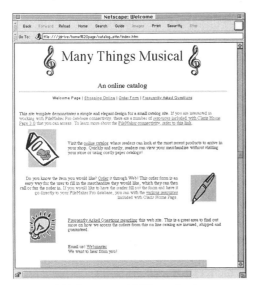

Figure 2. This is your raw HTML on a browser.

The Internet is changing our world—quickly. It has changed the nature of communication through e-mail and now, the nature of publishing through the World Wide Web. The Internet is becoming one of the grand populist forces of our time. All you need is a computer and access to this global network to put your own personal vision on display for all the world to see. Programs like Claris Home Page are making this process a whole lot easier.

Computers use programming code to do what they do, and HTML is the programming language of the World Wide Web (**Figure 1**). HTML-coded pages are the backbone of any World Wide Web site, and for a Web browser to view a site, the information must be in this format (**Figure 2**). While HTML is much simpler than other programming languages, it's still what we'd call a barrier to entry.

Home Page is designed to get you past that barrier, allowing you to build Web pages without knowing any HTML. Home Page is also a Web site publishing application, not just a page-building program. Its built-in tools take you from the basics of creating individual pages to the final steps of consolidating your site files and uploading them to your server. Sort of like a Swiss Army knife of the Web.

A Brief History of the Internet

The Internet comes up everywhere these days.

Commerce, the dissemination of knowledge, communications, many fundamental human interactions—all are changing purposefully as the Internet grows.

If you think that things are the same as they've always been, try cutting yourself off from your e-mail account for a few days and see what happens.

The Internet wasn't designed to turn out like this. It's been around since the sixties, when the U.S. Department of Defense set it up a "network of networks" so command operations could take place without a centralized switching point, which could be vulnerable in an attack. Originally, the Internet was a way to communicate through e-mail, or to transfer text-based information from place to play.

The Internet's glamour child, The World Wide Web, was born in the 1980's at the CERN laboratory in Switzerland for many of these same reasons. Physicists came up with the HTML language and protocols so their research projects could be shared and cross-referenced by scientists throughout the world.

As more and more people came online, however, the World Wide Web quickly took on a life of its own, and information published online grew at an astonishing rate. Finally, the Internet was hitting "the rest of us" and everyone from your corner store to your nephew had a Web site.

What HTML Does and Does Not Do

Claris Home page is here because of both what HTML does and doesn't do. HTML is a protocol, an agreed-upon set of communications rules. It's also a mark-up tool that tells browsers how to treat all your Web page elements, such as text, images, hyperlinks, e-mail addresses, and multimedia objects.

As mark-up languages go, HTML is an easy one to learn. Still, most people don't have the time or the inclination to learn it. It takes some effort and has its share of peculiarities. Still, HTML continues to grow and evolve, adding complexity and richness to its feature set.

Working with HTML, you can create an incredible web of pages, images, pieces of programming code, and spread it all over your computer. What HTML doesn't do is give you a way to organize it. HTML also is just a language. It doesn't come with a graphical tool to preview what you've done.

Hence, Home Page.

What Browsers Do

Web browsers—Netscape Navigator, Microsoft's Internet Explorer, AOL's browsers and others—access and interpret HTML pages so users can view them. Windows, Macintosh, and the various UNIX flavors all have browsers that display Web pages similarly. However, they do not necessarily display Web pages exactly the same (**Figure 3**), depending on the way the browser was set up and the individual quirks and limitations of each operating system.

Most of the world at this writing is using either Internet Explorer or Netscape Navigator.

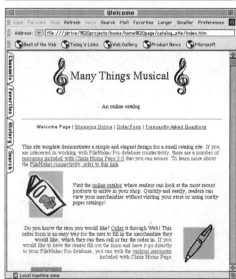

Figure 3. This is the same HTML page viewed in Netscape Navigator (top) and Microsoft's Internet Explorer (bottom). Look closely and you'll see a number of differences between them.

Verify Links
and References *Upload*
Consolidate

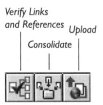

Figure 4. These three innocent-looking buttons are part of Home Page's unique arsenal of site-publishing tools.

Figure 5. Cut and paste and drag and drop text, images, and media from other applications and the files display immediately on your Home page screen.

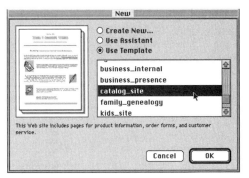

Figure 6. Choose from any one of Home Page's basic templates, then customize it with your own content.

Figure 7. Once you've set FTP options and consolidated your site files, you can upload them with the click of a button.

What Home Page Does

Home Page helps you to build simple to sophisticated Web pages without having to know HTML, lets you learn HTML along the way, and provides comprehensive site-publishing tools (**Figure 4**).

When programmers write HTML code in a text window, they repeatedly save the developing file and test it in a browser. This level of time commitment is beyond most non-programmers' attention spans, to say nothing of HTML's tendency to blow sky-high in the absence a single unclosed bracket. Then, when the pages are done, all site files must be gathered into a central location and uploaded using an FTP (File Transfer Protocol) application.

Home Page consolidates these steps by offering simple page-creation, site-assembly, and uploading tools in one package.

You'll work in an interactive WYSIWYG window that represents your Web page as it will display in a browser: entering text, dragging and dropping images and multimedia files directly onto the page and seeing your work as you go along (**Figure 5**).

Home Page offers a host of tools familiar to any user of word processing and graphics programs. Even if you've never designed a flyer or a newsletter, Home Page comes with a set of templates designed to meet many basic site needs (**Figure 6**), plus a set of *assistants* which walk you through the technical side of setting up entire sites.

When you're done building your site, Home Page assembles your site files with one easy step, and once you've set your FTP parameters, uploads the entire site to your server (**Figure 7**).

What this book does

The purpose of this book is to give you a comprehensive introduction to Home Page's tools and techniques. It's intended provide a quick, "hit the ground running" approach to learning by relying on visual examples and step-by-step instructions. Using the step-by-step instructions in this book—reading from cover to cover—will give you what it takes to make a professional Web site, whether you're making a home page for your hamster or a corporate site.

On the other hand, a book with an extensive index and a detailed table of contents practically invites skipping around from topic to topic as your need to know increases. For these more non-linear learners, this book is meant to be read with the thumbs, selecting topics as the need arises.

Figures show you what the text tells you.

Callouts highlight key screen features.

Good Web Practice sidebars give extra info about the Web.

Numbered steps walk you through the tasks.

Tips tell you things the program itself might not.

Thumb tabs help you locate sections quickly.

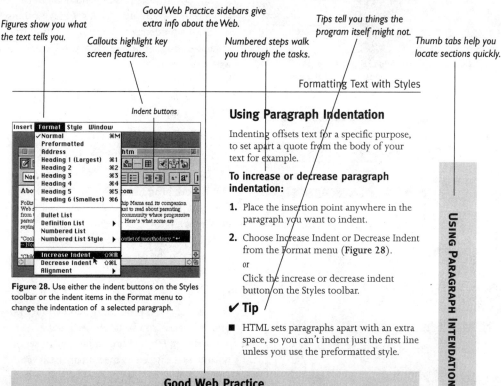

Indent buttons

Figure 28. Use either the indent buttons on the Styles toolbar or the indent items in the Format menu to change the indentation of a selected paragraph.

Formatting Text with Styles

Using Paragraph Indentation

Indenting offsets text for a specific purpose, to set apart a quote from the body of your text for example.

To increase or decrease paragraph indentation:

1. Place the insertion point anywhere in the paragraph you want to indent.

2. Choose Increase Indent or Decrease Indent from the Format menu (**Figure 28**).

   or

   Click the increase or decrease indent button on the Styles toolbar.

✔ Tip

- HTML sets paragraphs apart with an extra space, so you can't indent just the first line unless you use the preformatted style.

Good Web Practice

A word of warning.

Before we get into text formatting, a word of warning is in order. The World Wide Web has a feature that has rankled many a print designer (including this one). Despite your best efforts to make your pages look just so, the *client* system, on the receiving end, determines much of a page's look. This is especially true of text. If the client is set up to display all text in the font Spumoni, point size 24, that's how the end user views your pages. To complicate matters further, different browsers handle text differently, as do different platforms.

If your company logo happens to be in Times, somewhere on the World Wide Web someone will view it in Spumoni. If there is text you absolutely must have right, you'll need to make it an image file. We'll cover this in the next chapter.

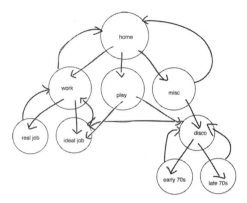

Figure 8. If you're starting from scratch, map out your pages and site structure before you begin.

About your pencil

The first step in designing a Web site is to sit down with a distinctly low-tech set of tools: a pencil and a blank piece of paper. Divide the material you want to put on the Web into topics, and assign a page to each topic. Then decide how to best present this material to the user. For most purposes, that will mean building a home page which is both the user's point of entry and the table of contents for the site. This process is called storyboarding.

With your pencil, plot the relationships between the topics in your pages, and then what linkages will be offered to other sites (**Figure 8**). When you see a logical structure developing, you'll know you're ready to begin. But first...

A final word

You won't be a good Web designer without first becoming a good Web user. Get on the Web as often as you can, and be critical of what you see, If something utterly gasses you, ask why. Determine what in a site's presentation causes you to return to a site again and again. Anybody with the tools and the time can make a Web site, but it takes commitment and talent to put up a site that actually contributes something to the Web's storehouse of knowledge.

THE BASICS

Figure 1. Who needs HTML? Home Page's WYSIWYG interface lets you manipulate text, links, images, movies, and sound files directly in the document window. In this chapter, you'll get a quick overview of the menus and tools you'll be working with.

Claris Home Page offers you a graphical approach to creating Web pages that is easy to learn. Like most Windows and Mac applications, Home Page gives you quick access to the tools you need through pull-down menus and toolbars with graphical buttons. Unlike most applications, however, if you want to get under the hood and fiddle with the underlying code, you can do so. The key is that Home Page doesn't let HTML code get in the way of your creative process.

In this chapter, you'll learn how to install the program and get a brief tour of the WYSIWYG (what you see is what you get) interface.

Installing and Launching Home Page

Now, let's cover some essentials. To get a look at the basics of Home Page you must first install the program and then launch a new page.

To Install Home Page:

1. Insert the installation CD in your computer's CD-ROM drive.

2. Double-click the installer icon.

3. Follow the directions.

The installation creates a folder containing the program icon, support files, and a read_me file describing the latest developments in the software. The CD also includes a copy of Adobe's Acrobat Reader and bonus art files.

To launch Home Page on a Mac:

1. Find the Claris Home Page folder on your hard drive. Double-click the folder to open it and locate the Claris Home Page 3.0 program icon (**Figure 2**).

2. Double-click the program icon.

To Launch Home Page in Windows 95 or Windows NT:

1. Click the Start button.

2. Choose the Claris Home Page icon from the program list.

A new, blank document—a "clean slate" Web page—opens in Edit Page mode (**Figure 3**).

✔ Tip

■ On a Mac, if you'll be using Home Page a lot, search your Macintosh Guide for the various ways you can make the program icon more accessible, such as putting an alias in the Apple menu or on your desktop.

Claris Home Page program icon

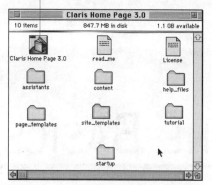

Figure 2. Along with the program icon, installing Home Page puts a lot of useful site-building files on your hard drive in the Claris Home Page folder.

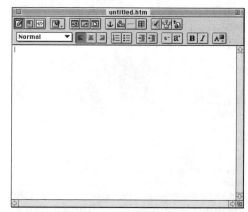

Figure 3. Home Page's first screen, a blank page, ready to be shaped into your Web masterpiece.

Figure 4. The top section of the File menu shows all your file-opening options.

Figure 5. Whether it's on your desktop or in a folder, you can just double-click a Home Page document icon to both launch the program and open the file.

Figure 6. Saving a document in a place that's easy to remember makes it easier to find when you want to open it again.

Opening and Saving a Document

By default Home Page opens a new page when you launch the program. There are two other ways to open a single-page document as well.

To open a new page:

Choose New Page from the File menu (**Figure 4**).

or

Press Ctrl N (Windows), or ⌘ N (Mac).

A blank page window appears.

To open an existing page:

Double-click a Home Page document icon you have saved on your hard drive. This will launch the program and open your saved Home Page document (**Figure 5**).

or

1. Choose Open from the File menu.

   or

   Press Ctrl O (Windows), or ⌘ O (Mac).

2. Find the document you want to open, and select Open from the dialog box (**Figure 6**).

To save your document:

With your page open, choose Save from the File menu.

OPENING AND SAVING A DOCUMENT

Home Page Menus

You have access to all the actions and commands in Home Page in the large assortment of menus above the toolbars. We'll cover most of them in detail (along with their corresponding toolbar buttons) later in the book.

Facts about Menus:

♦ Keyboard shortcuts appear to the right of some menu items (**Figure 7**). In this book, we'll just mention the basic ones. You'll need to keep an eye out for the rest, they're very handy!

♦ Menu items are grayed out when they're unavailable. For example, when you're in Preview mode, you'll see edit commands in the menus, but you won't be able to choose them.

♦ Commands with a triangle to their right (**Figure 8**) have submenus containing more choices.

♦ Three dots (an ellipsis) indicate that choosing a menu item calls up a dialog box (**Figure 9**).

♦ Check marks to the left of a menu item indicate current conditions, such as the mode in use (**Figure 10**). For example, before you customize your document, there's usually a check to the left of "Plain" under the Style menu, and in Edit mode you see a check mark next to Edit Page in the Window menu.

✔ Tip

■ Windows and Mac systems have slightly different keyboard shortcut schemes, though the principle is the same on both systems: you hold down one or more modifier keys and press another key.

Figure 7. Learn keyboard shortcuts by checking out the key combinations listed to the right of the menu item.

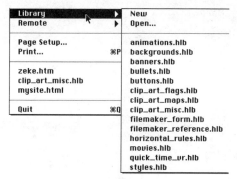

Figure 8. The triangle next to the Library menu item indicates that there is a submenu associated with it.

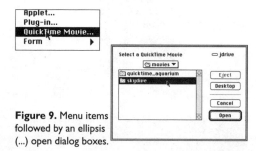

Figure 9. Menu items followed by an ellipsis (...) open dialog boxes.

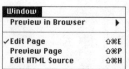

Figure 10. The Check next to Edit Page shows you're in Edit Page mode.

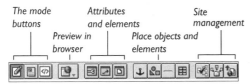

The mode buttons · Attributes and elements · Site management · Preview in browser · Place objects and elements

Figure 11. The buttons on the basic toolbar are grouped according to their function.

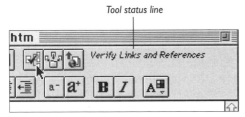

Tool status line

Figure 12. Stumped about what a button does? Just place the cursor over the button without clicking, and the button's name appears in the Tool Status line.

The Basic Toolbar

The Basic toolbar is divided into sections of buttons grouped according to their functions. Windows users will find the first four buttons on the left familiar from many other Windows programs. They are New File, Open File, Save File, and Print. These buttons are not on the Mac version of the program.

From there, the buttons are the same on both the Mac and Windows versions of Home Page (**Figure 11**). **Table 1** gives the name and utility of each button.

✔ Tips

■ To find out the name of a tool quickly, place your cursor over the button without clicking. The button's name appears in the Tool Status line to the right of the Basic toolbar (**Figure 12**).

■ In the Windows version of Home Page, you can elect to turn off this feature by selecting Hide Tooltips from the Help menu.

Table 1. The Basic toolbar buttons

BUTTON	BUTTON NAME	WHAT IT DOES	BUTTON	BUTTON NAME	WHAT IT DOES
	Edit Page Mode	Allows you to enter text and other content.		Insert Anchor	Defines hypertext links that jump to specific parts of pages within your Web site.
	Preview Page Mode	Shows an approximation of your page as it will appear in a browser.		Insert Image	Opens a dialog box with options for placing images on your pages.
	Edit HTML Mode	Allows you to modify the HTML code of your file.		Insert Horizontal Rule	Places a horizontal rule on your page.
	Preview in Browser	Displays your page in your browser.		Insert Table	Inserts a table.
	Object Editor	Modifies objects, such as images, anchors, tables, applets, frames, and rules.		Verify Links and References	Checks that all links, images and other files exist in a form that can be uploaded.
	Link Editor	Creates and edits links, both to pages and e-mail addresses.		Consolidate	Places all referenced images and other objects into one folder along with your HTML files.
	Document Options	Sets page attributes such as background color, link and text colors, and page title.		Upload	Sends your finished work to your server.

THE BASIC TOOLBAR

Home Page View Modes

Home Page offers you three viewing options, called *modes*. Each mode serves a different purpose, displaying the same information in different ways. *Edit Page* mode is for entering and editing text and other material. *Preview Page* mode is for checking links among your pages and showing an approximation of what your page will look like in a browser (**Figure 13**).

Edit HTML Source mode is for viewing all the HTML code Home Page writes for you! (**Figure 14**) You can use Source mode to edit and debug a page in HTML, if you decide to learn this language.

To view your page in the different modes:

1. Open a Home Page document.

2. Select the different modes on the basic toolbar (**Figure 15**).

   or

   Choose a mode from the Window menu (**Figure 16**).

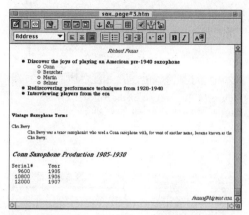

Figure 13. Edit Page mode is for entering and editing text and other content. Preview mode looks the same but you cannot edit or insert material, nor can you test links.

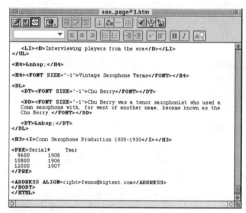

Figure 14. Edit HTML Source mode shows you the code that's being generated by your WYSIWYG (What You See Is What You Get) actions in Edit Page mode.

Figure 15. Three view mode buttons: Edit Page, Preview Page, and Edit HTML Source.

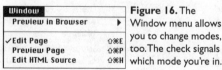

Figure 16. The Window menu allows you to change modes, too. The check signals which mode you're in.

Figure 17. Preview in Browser opens the page you're working on in an external Web browser.

Good Web Practice

Check your work in a browser.

For best results publishing pages to the Web, it's a good idea to check your work in both dominant Web browsers. That means, of course, you'll have to obtain and install both Netscape and Explorer on your computer. It's a small price to pay to assure good, predictable results on most visitors' systems.

Previewing Pages in a Browser

Home Page's modes allow you different ways to view your work. The program also allows you an external option, one that uses programs other than Home Page. The *Preview in Browser* mode displays your page in Microsoft Internet Explorer, Netscape Navigator, or both.

When we discuss frames further in Chapter 8, you'll learn about yet another mode, *Frame Edit*, which has its own set of toolbars.

To view your page in a browser:

1. Open a Home Page document.

2. Click the Preview in Browser button in the basic toolbar (**Figure 17**), and choose one of the browsers offered.

   or

   Choose Preview in Browser from the Window menu and choose one or both browsers.

✔ Tips

■ The first time you choose an item from the Preview in Browser button's drop-down list, Home Page searches for the browser on your hard drive. If it can't find your browser, the program prompts you for its location.

■ Web browsers are RAM-hungry, but if you have enough memory, toggle back and forth between Home Page and your browser to check how your page displays as you go along. Use the standard methods: Ctrl Alt in Windows, or on the Mac, toggle from the active program list in the upper right corner of your screen.

PREVIEWING PAGES IN A BROWSER

Object Editors

Anything you put on a page using Claris Home Page is an *object*. Home Page's Object Editors allow you a convenient way to view and edit object properties (also called *attributes*).

To open the Object Editor:

1. Open a Home Page document that has some content and images in it.

2. Select an object, such as an image.

3. Click the Object Editor button on the Styles toolbar (**Figure 18**).

   or

   You can also open Object Editor palettes by double-clicking on the object you wish to change.

The Object Editor for the selected object opens up, and you can view and change any of the attributes of the selected object (**Figure 19**).

✔ Tips

- You can only use the Object Editors in Edit mode, not in Preview mode.

- If no object is selected in the document window, the Object Editor displays the message shown in **Figure 20**. Leave this blank palette open and it will display the attributes of any object you select.

- You can move Object Editor palettes out of your way by clicking and dragging their title bar.

We'll deal with the other Object Editor palettes in later chapters that cover specific objects in depth.

Figure 18. The Object Editor button.

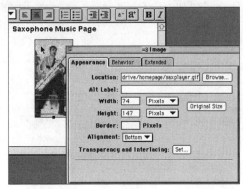

Figure 19. This is an Object Editor in action. With the image selected, you can view and change almost every attribute of the image.

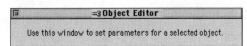

Figure 20. When the Object Editor is open but no objects are selected, this message appears.

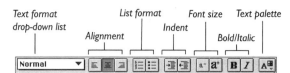

Text format drop-down list *List format* *Alignment* *Indent* *Font size* *Text palette* *Bold/Italic*

Figure 21. The Styles toolbar gives you easy access to text and image formatting tools.

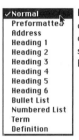

Figure 22. The text format drop-down menu lets you change the characteristics of selected text by applying HTML styles.

Figure 23. Click and hold the Text Palette button to reveal the palette used to choose the color of selected text.

The Styles Toolbar

Although you can use some of its tools for images, the Styles toolbar (**Figure 21**) is primarily designed to help you format text.

Table 2 identifies each tool and describes what it does. The Styles toolbar has two tools that work differently from the other command buttons. Leftmost on the Styles toolbar is a drop-down list of paragraph formats (**Figure 22**). Pull down and select one of these formats to change the characteristics of a selected paragraph. The last button on the Styles toolbar is another drop-down menu that gives you options for changing the color of selected text (**Figure 23**).

Table 2. The Styles toolbar buttons

Tool	Name	What it does	Tool	Name	What it does
Normal ▾	Paragraph Format drop-down list	Applies a style to text.	⊞	Add Indent	Indents text.
≣	Left Align	Aligns text to the left.	⊟	Remove Indent	Removes indent from text.
≣	Center Align	Aligns text to the center.	a⁻	Decrease Text Size	Decreases the size of text.
≣	Right Align	Aligns text to the right.	a⁺	Increase Text Size	Increases the size of text.
≣	Numbered List	Creates a numbered list.	B	Bold	Boldfaces text.
≣	Bulleted List	Creates a bulleted list.	I	Italics	Italicizes text.
			A	Color	Applies a color to selected text.

Getting Help

Claris Home Page includes an extensive set of indexed and searchable Help files.

To open and use Help:

1. Click and hold the Question Mark icon in the upper-right corner of your screen (**Figure 24**).

2. Choose the menu item you want to learn about, or choose Contents or Index from the drop-down menu for a more complete display of help topics (**Figures 25 and 26**).

   After you've chosen a topic, you'll see information about it, and often hyperlinks to related topics as well.

3. Explore!

✔ Tips

- For a useful, self-paced tutorial, choose Tutorial from the Help menu.

- Choose Jump Start from the Help menu for a step-by-step outline of help and tutorial files you can use to create basic and advanced Web sites with Home Page.

Figure 24. Clicking and holding on the question mark icon displays the extensive Help menu.

Figure 25. Home Page Help contents lets you choose from preselected topics.

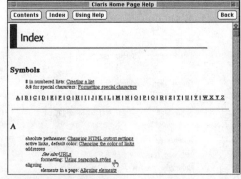

Figure 26. The Help Index has a complete list of terms that you can find help on.

ENTERING AND EDITING TEXT

Figure 1. You can copy and paste (or drag and drop) text from word processing, page layout, and other documents, into your Home Page Edit Page window.

In Claris Home Page, working with the text in your Web documents is as easy as using your favorite word processing application. In fact, you can copy (or sometimes, drag and drop) text directly from a word processing document into your Web page, then use Home Page's mark-up tools to format it (**Figure 1**).

This chapter focuses on basic text operations such as entering, deleting, moving, and copying text; in the next chapter you'll learn how to spruce it up with formatting.

Entering Text

Anyone who uses a word processor is familiar with the insertion point, the blinking character on the screen that tells you where the cursor is in your document. In the document window, the insertion point shows you where the text you type will show up. Use the mouse or arrow keys to place the I-beam cursor (**Figure 2**) where you want the insertion point to be, then click the mouse button to place the insertion on your page.

To enter text directly into your Web page:

1. Open a Home Page document.

2. Position the insertion point by clicking on your page.

If you are working in a new, blank document window, the insertion point will be in the upper left corner of the screen. Once you've placed objects (text, images, tables, and so forth) you'll have the option of placing your cursor anywhere around them.

3. Start typing.

✔ Tips

■ All editing must take place in Edit mode (**Figure 3**).

■ Press ⎡Enter⎤ (Windows) or ⎡Return⎤ (Mac) to start a new paragraph. Web pages display a line space between paragraphs.

■ As with a word processor, you can insert text in the middle of existing text by placing your cursor where you'd like to add new material and typing or pasting it in.

■ You won't see any hyphenation while you are typing text. The World Wide Web doesn't currently support text hyphenation.

■ When you enter text, it breaks (or, *wraps*) when it reaches the edge of your document window.

Insertion point

I-Beam cursor

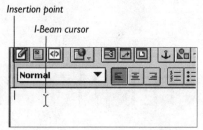

Figure 2. The insertion point is located in the upper left corner of a new document. The I-beam cursor indicates the mouse's position.

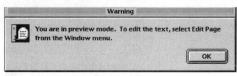

Figure 3. If you try to enter text in Preview mode, you get this error message.

&#169;	© (Copyright) [© ©]
&#170;	ª (Feminine ordinal) [ª &ordf]
&#171;	« (Left angle quote, guillemotleft) [« &laquo]
&#172;	¬ (Not sign) [¬ &not]

Figure 4. You'll see a list of symbols and their HTML code equivalents when you choose HTML Code from the Insert Menu.

The contents of this web page are [image] 1997, by Zeke, Inc.

Figure 5. This placeholder shows you where you've inserted HTML code that will appear as a symbol in the browser window.

Figure 6. Fill in the code in the HTML Code window and click to close the box when done.

The contents of this web page are ©1997, by Zeke, Inc.

Figure 7. After you save and reopen your file, the character displays correctly.

Special Characters

HTML uses a number of characters such as brackets, slashes, and exclamation points in its code to designate how your pages will function. Since you'll most likely want to use characters like these in the text of your Web pages too, HTML provides a set of codes that read and display special characters correctly when viewed within a Web browser.

To insert a special character:

1. Choose Special Characters from the Help menu. If you need to, adjust the size of your document window so you can have both it and the Help window open.

2. Scroll through the list of characters until you find the one you're looking for. Write down the HTML code for the special character(s) (**Figure 4**), or highlight and copy the text string.

   Note that all codes begin with an ampersand and a number sign (#), end with a semicolon (;), and have a two- or three-digit number in the middle.

3. Back in your Home Page document, place the insertion point in the text where you want to insert the special character, and choose HTML Code from the Insert menu.

   A placeholder like the one shown in **Figure 5** appears in the text, and the HTML Code Object Editor dialog box opens.

4. Enter or paste the special character code into the HTML Code field (**Figure 6**), and close the HTML Code Object Editor dialog box.

6. Click the Edit HTML Source button, then go back to Edit Page mode. The special character displays correctly (**Figure 7**).

INSERTING SPECIAL CHARACTERS

Selecting Text

Many operations require you to select groups of words: sentences, paragraphs, and larger blocks. Besides clicking and dragging the cursor while holding down the mouse button to highlight text, there are several time-saving techniques for selecting text.

To shift-select text:

1. Place the insertion point at either the beginning or the end of the text block you want to select.

2. Click your mouse button (left button for Windows).

3. Press and hold down the (Shift) key.

4. Place the insertion point at the other end of the text block you want to select.

5. Click your mouse button again. The text in the selection block is now highlighted.

✔ Tips

Another handy text-selection shortcut is to multiple-click words and paragraphs.

- To select a word, place the insertion point anywhere in the word and double-click. The word is now highlighted.

- To select an entire paragraph, place the insertion point anywhere in the paragraph and triple-click. The paragraph is now selected.

- To select the entire contents of a document, choose Select All from the Edit menu.

Figure 8. Selected text appears against a shaded background.

Figure 9. The space after the first line indicates a new paragraph, bent arrows at the end of the second two lines on this page show line breaks that don't begin new paragraphs.

Editing Text

If you've used a word processor, or your computer for that matter, you already know the very basic word processing techniques: placing your cursor where you want to enter text, pressing Enter (Windows), or Return (Mac) to insert a paragraph break, using Backspace (Windows), or Delete (Mac) to delete text, and so on. Following are a couple of lesser-known actions.

To insert a line break without starting a new paragraph:

1. Move the insertion point to the left of the character you want to start the new line.

2. Press Shift Enter (Windows) or Shift Return (Mac) (**Figure 9**).

To delete text to the right of the insertion point one character at a time:

1. Position the cursor to the left of the character(s) you wish to delete.

2. Press Delete (Windows), ⌦ (Mac).

To remove a line break:

Place the insertion point at the beginning of the text line below the line break symbol (the arrow) and press Delete.

EDITING TEXT

15

Working with Selected Text

Once you select a block of text, you can perform a number of operations on it (more old favorites from the word processing arena). Among the most useful are: overwrite, copy and paste, cut and paste, and drag and drop.

To overwrite text:

1. Select a text block you wish to replace.

2. Type the new text. The old text block will be deleted and the new text will take its place.

To copy and paste text:

1. Select the text block you wish to copy.

2. Choose Copy from the Edit menu or press Ctrl C (Windows), ⌘ C (Mac).
A copy of the selected text is now in your computer's memory.

3. Place the insertion point where you want to insert the text block.

4. Choose Paste from the Edit menu (**Figure 10**) or press Ctrl V (Windows), ⌘ V (Mac).
This pastes the text at insertion point.

To cut and paste text:

1. Select the text block you wish to move.

2. Select Cut from the Edit menu or press Ctrl X (Windows), ⌘ X (Mac).
A copy of the selected text is now in your computer's memory, and the text has been deleted from your document.

3. Place the insertion point where you want to insert the text block.

4. Select Paste from the Edit menu, or press Ctrl V (Windows), ⌘ V (Mac).
The text you cut is now pasted in at the insertion point.

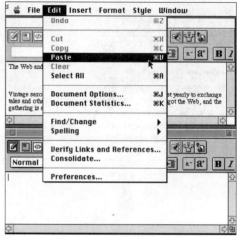

Figure 10. You can copy text from almost any application and paste it into your Home Page document.

✔ Tips

■ With Copy and Paste, the original selected text stays in its position. You are adding an identical text block elsewhere without destroying the original material.

■ The text you copy stays in your computer's memory (on the *clipboard*) until another selection replaces it, or until you shut off your computer. This means you can use the Paste command again at another location, in another document, or even in a document in another application, subject to certain restrictions.

■ If you find that you've cut text mistakenly, use Paste to put it back where it belongs, or choose Undo from the Edit menu (more on Undo later in this chapter).

WORKING WITH SELECTED TEXT

Drag and Drop

Drag-and-drop editing is the latest technique for copying text and moving it—using only your mouse—around a page, between documents, or between applications that support this functionality.

To copy or move text using drag and drop:

1. Select the text you want to copy.

2. Place your cursor anywhere within the selected text block. The mouse pointer, usually an I-beam cursor, becomes an arrow.

3. Click and hold down the mouse button. You have now "lifted" a copy of the selected text from the page.

4. Continuing to hold down the mouse button, move the arrow to another location in your document window, to another document window, or to a window in any application that supports drag and drop.

   In the new location, the cursor becomes an insertion point (**Figure 11**).

5. Place the insertion point where you want to insert the text, and release the mouse button.

✔ Tip

■ To use drag and drop to copy text and paste it in a new location while leaving the original text block intact, hold down [Ctrl] (Windows) or [Option] (Mac) while moving the cursor to a new location.

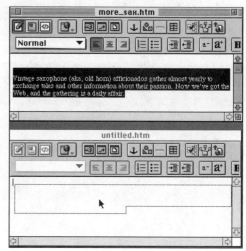

Figure 11. Dragging text from the top window into the bottom window.

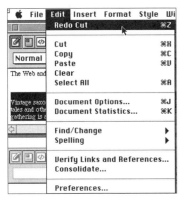

Figure 12. After you undo a cut, the Undo menu item becomes a Redo menu item.

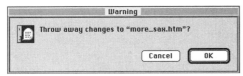

Figure 13. After choosing Revert from the File menu, you've got one last chance to change your mind about it.

Undo, Redo, and Revert

There comes a time in every document's history when you wish you hadn't made some boneheaded move—deleting important text, moving an image where it looks just awful—the possibilities are endless. Luckily, there are two ways around human error in Home Page: Undo and Revert.

To undo:

After your regrettable move and before you do anything else, choose Undo from the Edit menu, or press [Ctrl] [Z] (Windows) or [⌘] [Z] (Mac).

(Don't you wish we had something like this in life?)

To redo:

If the last action you performed was an Undo, the Undo menu item becomes the Redo menu item. Choose this item to undo your undo.

This also gives you information about what your last action was. In **Figure 12,** you can see that the Undo/Redo command would reverse a cut.

When you've undone all you can undo and you still want to go back to the good old days before you made a bunch of silly changes to your document, you also have the option of reverting to the version you saved last.

To revert to the last saved version:

1. Choose Revert from the File menu.

    A dialog box asks if you want to throw away all the changes you've made to your document since you last saved (**Figure 13**).

2. Click OK.

UNDO, REDO, AND REVERT

✔ Tips

- Undo only undoes the last action you've taken.

- If Undo is unavailable (for example, if your last action was saving your document), it will be grayed out. If you attempt to use the keyboard shortcut, the computer will beep.

- When a button in a dialog box is highlighted (like the OK button in **Figure 13**), you can press Enter (Windows), Return (Mac) to select it.

- When you revert, you lose *all* the changes you've made to your document since the last save, both good and bad.

Good Web Practice

Save, Save, Save!

Well, this isn't necessarily Web practice exclusively, but as with other computer projects that you can spend hours on, remember to save your work often. Practice the keyboard shortcut, Ctrl S (Windows) or ⌘ S (Mac), until you can perform it without looking.

Figure 14. The Find/Change dialog box is used to search for and replace text.

Figure 15. Keep selecting Find Next to highlight each instance of your word one by one.

Figure 16. Find/Change highlights found text in your document window.

Table 1. Find/Change dialog box options

BUTTON	WHAT IT DOES
Change	Changes the highlighted text.
Change All	Changes all occurrences of the text in your document.
Change, Find	Changes the occurrence and displays the next to see if you want to change that one, too.
Find Next	Goes to the next occurrence without changing it.

Find/Change Text Operations

Nothing in your document window can hide for long from Home Page's Find and Change tools. The Find/Change dialog box (**Figure 14**) helps you locate text blocks of any length, HTML code, Web addresses (URLs), and more.

To find text:

1. Select Find/Change from the Edit menu or press [Ctrl] [F] (Windows), [⌘] [F] (Mac). This opens the Find/Change dialog box.

2. Type the text you're looking for into the Find text box.

3. Select the Find Next button to begin searching (**Figure 15**).
   The search highlights the found word in your document behind the dialog box (**Figure 16**).

4. Close the Find/Change dialog box when you're done.

To change text:

1. Select Find/Change from the Edit menu.

2. Type the text you want to change into the Find text box.

3. Type the replacement text into the Change To text box.

4. Click the Find Next button.

5. When Find/Change locates the text you are looking for, you can choose from the options shown in **Table 1,** which appear as buttons at the bottom of the dialog box.

6. Close the Find/Change dialog box.

✔ Tip

■ If the document window is hidden by the Find/Change dialog box, click and hold the title bar to move it.

Defining Find/Change Operations

Home Page offers an at first bewildering number of options for refining and broadening Find/Change operations. Once you learn how to use them, you'll find them quite helpful.

Home Page's find/change options:

♦ The Search In drop-down list (**Figure 17**) lets you choose which document windows Home Page searches.

♦ The Mode drop-down list (**Figure 18**) allows you to search either in Edit mode or in raw HTML.

Four check boxes (**Figure 19**) define search criteria:

♦ The Case Sensitive check box limits matched words to the exact uppercase and lowercase spelling.

♦ The Whole Word check box narrows matches to text that does not include any characters except the ones in the Find field. For example, with this box checked, a search for the word *sting* wouldn't find *lasting*.

♦ The Search Backwards check box reverses the default search direction from below the insertion point to above it.

♦ If you start checking your document in the middle, the Wrap Around check box scans the entire document after it reaches the end.

✔ Tips

■ The entire bottom row of the Find/Change dialog box is grayed out until you type text into the Find text box.

■ You can also use the Find/Change operation to delete text. Enter the text to be deleted in the Find text box and leave the Change To text box empty. This replaces the Find text with nothing.

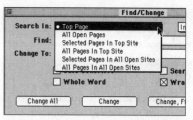

Figure 17. With the Search In drop-down list, you can search an entire site's files.

Figure 18. The Mode drop-down list specifies a search in Edit mode or HTML mode.

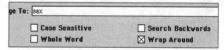

Figure 19. Four check boxes help you refine your text searches.

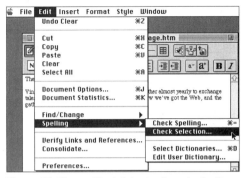

Figure 20. Choose Check Selection from the Spelling submenu to check the spelling of selected text.

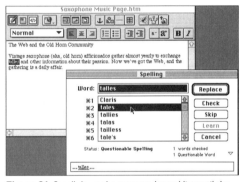

Figure 21. Scroll down the suggested word list until the correct spelling is highlighted, then select Replace.

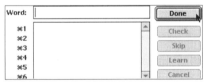

Figure 22. The Done button appears only when you've dealt with all suspect words.

Good Web Practice

Spelling

No spelling checker is even close to perfect. Checking spelling is just a process of comparing document words with dictionary lists. While it may catch *hte*, your spelling checker doesn't know the difference between *there* and *their*, *its* and *it's*. There's no substitute for human knowledge of grammar and vocabulary—yet.

Using the Spelling Checker

Nothing's more annoying than a Web site with spelling errors, yet it's all too common. Home Page has a powerful and flexible spelling checker that uses two dictionaries, either US English or UK English, and User Dictionary. User Dictionary contains all the words you "teach" the dictionary. As we will soon learn, you may add custom user dictionaries as well.

To check spelling of a single word, a block of text, or the entire document:

1. Select a word, text block, or your entire document.

2. Choose Spelling from the Tools menu (Windows) or Edit menu (Mac), then choose Check Selection from the resulting submenu (**Figure 20**).

3. If the spelling checker finds the word misspelled, it offers a series of alternate spellings (**Figure 21**). Find the correct one and select Replace.

   or

   Press the keyboard shortcut to the left of the correct word.

4. If the word is spelled correctly, select Skip to skip the word or Learn to add the word to your user dictionary.

5. If none of the words is correct, you can type in the correct word in the Word field, then select Replace.

6. When you're finished, click Done (**Figure 22**).

7. To close the Spelling dialog box without making any changes, select Cancel.

✔ Tip

■ Press Ctrl A (Windows) or ⌘ A (Mac) to select the entire document.

Using Home Page Dictionaries

If you have projects that use different sets of terms—say, medical terms or baseball players' names—Home Page can set up separate dictionaries that you can use for each project.

To create a new user dictionary:

1. Choose Spelling from the Tools menu (Windows) or the Edit menu (Mac) and choose Select Dictionaries from the resulting submenu (**Figure 23**).

2. Choose User Dictionary from the Select Dictionary Type drop-down list (**Figure 24**). The Select Dictionary Type dialog box appears.

3. On the Mac select New to bring up a Save As dialog box. Name the new user dictionary (**Figure 25**) and select Save. In Windows, enter the name of the dictionary in the File Name box, then select New. With the new dictionary's name highlighted, select Open.

✔ Tip

- The new user dictionary you have just set up will function along with the main dictionary as the reference for spelling checks until you select another.

To change dictionaries:

1. Choose Spelling from the Tools menu (Windows) or the Edit menu (Mac), choose Select Dictionaries from the resulting submenu (**Figure 23**), and choose either the Main (to change to and from UK and US English) or User Dictionary from the Select Dictionary Type drop-down list.

2. Scroll through the list of Dictionaries and choose one with the Select button (**Figure 26**). The Currently Selected Dictionary displays at the bottom of the Select Dictionary Type dialog box, and click Done.

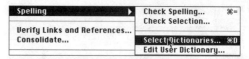

Figure 23. Access your Dictionary dialog boxes through the Spelling submenus.

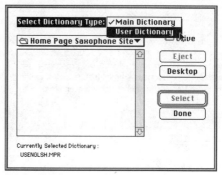

Figure 24. You can create as many new user dictionaries as you want to for your different Home Page sites and documents.

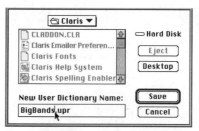

Figure 25. Choose a name for your dictionary that makes it clear which document it goes with.

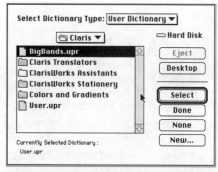

Figure 26. Select a user dictionary from the list in your Claris folder.

Figure 27. Choose Edit User Dictionary from the Spelling menu to make changes or additions to existing user dictionaries.

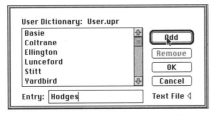

Figure 28. Keep entering words and clicking Add to add new terms to your user dictionary.

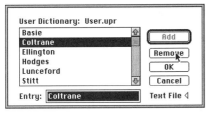

Figure 29. Remove all the words you want to by clicking the Remove button.

Modifying a User Dictionary

The Add function in the spelling checker adds words to your user dictionary. You can also add words when you are not performing a spelling check.

There are also times when you'll want to remove custom words from your user dictionary, or export the words in a custom dictionary to use elsewhere.

To add a word to a user dictionary:

1. Choose Spelling from the Tools menu (Windows) or the Edit menu (Mac), then choose Edit User Dictionary from the resulting submenu (**Figure 27**).

2. Type the word you want to add in the Entry text box, then select Add (**Figure 28**).

3. When finished entering terms, click OK.

✔ Tip

■ A word that your spelling checker "learns" when you add it to the User Dictionary remains there even after you quit the program.

To delete a word from a user dictionary:

1. Choose Spelling from the Tools menu (Windows) or Edit menu (Mac), then choose Edit User Dictionary from the resulting submenu.

2. Scroll through the word list, locate the word you want to remove, and select Remove (**Figure 29**).

3. When finished deleting items, select OK.

MODIFYING A USER DICTIONARY

To import a list of words in text format to a user dictionary:

1. Choose Spelling from the Tools menu (Windows) or the Edit menu (Mac), then choose Edit User Dictionary from the resulting submenu.

2. Click the triangle next to the words *Text File*. The dialog box increases in size.

3. Select Import (**Figure 30**). The words you import into the user dictionary need to be in text file format.

4. In the resulting dialog box, locate the text file you'd like to import into the user dictionary, and click OK.

✔ Tip

■ To save a file in text format, create or open it in a word processing application, choose Save As from the File menu, and select the Save as Text Only document option (**Figure 31**).

To export a list of words from a user dictionary to a text file:

1. Choose Spelling from the Tools menu (Windows) or the Edit menu (Mac), then choose Edit User Dictionary from the resulting submenu.

2. Click the triangle next to the words *Text File*. The dialog box increases in size.

3. Click Export (**Figure 32**), and use the resulting dialog box to select where you want to save your dictionary text file. Name the Export file and click Save (**Figure 33**).

4. Select OK in the User Dictionary dialog box to return to your work.

Figure 30. Import a word list from a text application to make spell checking easier.

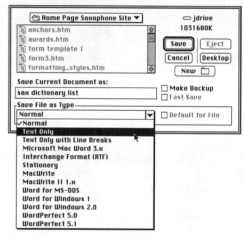

Figure 31. Save your word list as text only to import it.

Figure 32. Exporting your user dictionary words.

Figure 33. Save the word list to your hard drive.

Formatting

Text with Styles

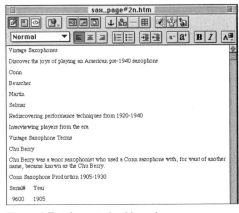

Figure 1. Text formatted as Normal.

Figure 2. Same text, various styles applied.

When you enter text in a Home Page document or paste it in from another application, it starts out looking pretty plain (**Figure 1**). In style terminology, it's called Normal.

To liven up your pages, distinguish text elements from each other, and create visual order, you'll want to apply some styles (**Figure 2**).

There are two kinds of text formatting options: *paragraph styles* and *character styles*. They control font size and style, text alignment and indentation, and can automatically organize your text into bulleted and numbered lists with just a single action—applying some style.

About Paragraph Formatting

Paragraph formats are controlled in HTML with **styles**. Styles apply to an entire paragraph's text. They control font size and spacing with headings, preformatted, and address styles; and indentation and alignment with numbered and bulleted lists, terms, and definitions. All the paragraph styles described in this section are applied in essentially the same way.

To apply a paragraph style:

1. Place the insertion point anywhere in the paragraph you wish to format.

2. Choose a style from the Format menu (**Figure 3**) or from the drop-down menu on the Styles toolbar (**Figure 4**)

   or

   Click one of the Styles toolbar buttons (**Figure 5**).

To remove a paragraph style:

1. Place the insertion point anywhere in the paragraph text.

2. Choose Normal from the Format menu or from the drop-down menu in the Styles toolbar.

✔ Tip

■ Remember, paragraphs are text blocks of any length set apart by carriage returns.

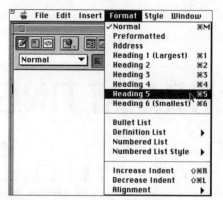

Figure 3. The Format menu includes text formatting and paragraph style options.

Figure 4. The Styles toolbar drop-down menu lists only paragraph style choices.

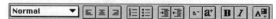

Figure 5. The handy Styles toolbar puts some paragraph and text formatting just a click away.

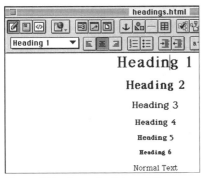

Figure 6. Heading styles 1 through 3 are larger than Normal, 4 is the same size as Normal, and 5 and 6 are smaller than Normal.

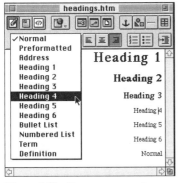

Figure 7. Headings are easy to change with the Styles drop-down menu.

Applying a Heading Style

There are six different levels of paragraph heading styles, often used to organize your page with headlines, titles, subtitles, and the like. Each one displays in bold and is followed by an automatic paragraph return.

Heading font and point size are determined by individual browser configuration on the viewer end, so in the Home Page window, they are only sized relative to the default size of the browser's Normal style (**Figure 6**).

To apply a heading style:

1. Place the insertion point anywhere in the text block you want to style as a heading.

2. Choose a heading from either the Format menu or the drop-down menu in the Styles toolbar (**Figure 7**).

✔ Tips

- If you know a little HTML, you'll find it easy to remember the keyboard shortcuts for Headings. [Alt] [1] (Windows) or [⌘] [1] (Mac) correspond to the HTML tag <H1> for level 1 headings, and so on through the six available Heading tags.

- Headings can also include bold and italics. You'll learn how to apply selected character styles later in this chapter.

Using Preformatted Text

Preformatted text displays in a mono-spaced font, typically Courier. Each character in a monospaced font is the same width, so you can enter multiple spaces to simulate tab stops in charts and simple tables.

To create a table with preformatted style:

1. Enter the text you want to format as a table, typing only one space between column entries (**Figure 8**).

2. Highlight the entire block of text.

3. Choose Preformatted from the Format menu (**Figure 9**) or from the drop-down menu in the Styles toolbar.

4. Position the cursor and press the space bar where you want to add space between your columns (**Figure 10**).

✔ Tips

- Normal style does not recognize multiple spaces, so text must be styled as preformatted before multiple character spaces will show up.

- Since the advent of HTML Tables (see Chapter 8), it has become less and less common to present information using the Preformatted style.

Figure 8. Enter all your text for preformatting first without adding spaces.

Figure 9. After you've entered your table data, choose the Preformatted text style.

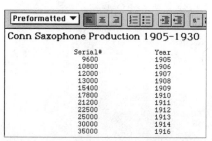

Figure 10. Using Preformatted style, your text spacing will look just like it does on your screen.

Figure 11. The byline and *for more information…* text on this page is styled as an address and centered using paragraph alignment.

Figure 12. Don't forget to look for keyboard shortcuts when you choose a style from the Format menu.

Applying the Address Style

The Address style applies the italic version of Normal, with a space above and below text, to display items like e-mail addresses, mailing addresses, or bylines on your Web page (**Figure 11**). You can use it however you want; it's a handy way to offset an italicized line from the body text of your document.

To apply the address style:

1. Place the insertion point anywhere in the text you want to style as an address.

2. Choose Address from the Format menu (**Figure 12**) or from the drop-down menu in the Styles toolbar.

APPLYING THE ADDRESS STYLE

Creating Bulleted Lists

Commonly used in Web pages, bulleted lists use the browser's bullet character (•) to set apart listed items. Bulleted lists have no extra spaces between entries (**Figure 13**).

To create a bulleted list:

1. In Edit mode, type or paste in the list items, inserting paragraph returns between them.

2. Select the entire list (**Figure 14**), and choose Bullet List from the Format menu or from the drop-down list on the Styles toolbar.

   or

   Click the Make Bullet List Entry button on the Styles toolbar (**Figure 15**).

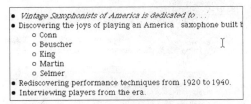

Figure 13. Bullet lists are common on the Web—and easily created in Home Page.

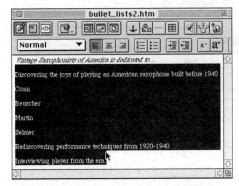

Figure 14. Type in the items for your bulleted list and highlight them, and…

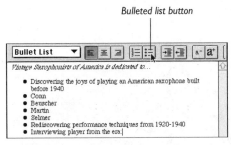

Figure 15. …click the Make Bullet List Entry button on the Styles toolbar to automatically apply the bulleted list style.

Figure 16. You have five styles to choose from when you display information in a Numbered List.

Figure 17. In Edit mode, five different placeholders represent the filing number styles.

Styles toolbar drop-down list

Numbered list button

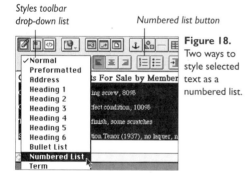

Figure 18. Two ways to style selected text as a numbered list.

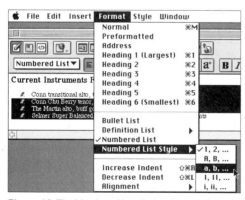

Figure 19. The Numbered List Style submenu shows you what number characters you have to choose from.

Creating Numbered Lists

Numbered Lists precede items with characters of various styles in ascending order: roman numerals (I, II, III... or i, ii, iii...), arabic numerals (1, 2, 3...), or letters (a, b, c... or A, B, C...) (**Figure 16**). In Edit mode, numbered lists are displayed without their numbers; they use a placeholder character until you view the list in Preview or Preview in Browser mode (**Figure 17**).

To create a numbered list:

1. Type or paste in the list items in Edit mode, inserting paragraph returns between them.

2. Select the entire list, and choose Numbered List from the Format menu or from the drop-down list on the Styles toolbar (**Figure 18**).

   or

   Click the Make Numbered List Entry button on the Styles toolbar.

To change number character style:

Select your entire numbered list, and choose Numbered List Style from the Format menu and select a character style from the resulting submenu (**Figure 19**).

✔ Tip

- You can reorder a numbered list by using drag and drop or cut and paste. When you do, the numbering will change to reflect the new list order.

Creating Nested Lists

Nested Lists are "lists within lists," where an indent indicates a series of list items that are subcategories of a main list item. You can use this feature with both bulleted and numbered lists.

To create a nested list:

1. If you haven't already, enter your list—main categories and subcategories—starting each item on a new line (**Figure 20**).

2. Format the entire list—including the subcategories—as a bulleted or numbered list (*see pages 32 and 33*).

3. Highlight the subcategories of your list (**Figure 21**).

4. Nest the subcategories by either selecting Increase Indent from the Format Menu, or clicking the Increase Indent button on the Styles toolbar. (See the indenting section in this chapter for more on indenting text).

   The bullet style of subcategories changes, and the nested numbered list items will have their own numerical sequence (**Figure 22**).

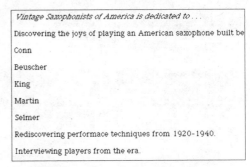

Figure 20. Enter all your list items first without worrying about indenting subcategories.

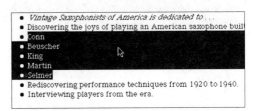

Figure 21. Highlight the subcategories and indent them to make a nested list.

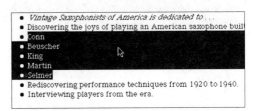

Figure 22. Nested items in a bullet list are distinguished by open bullets.

CREATING NESTED LISTS

```
Vintage Saxophone terms

Chu Berry
        Chu Berry was a tenor saxophonist who used a model of C
        which, for want of another name, was called the Chu Berry
Transitional
        The Transitional model Conns were built between the Chu
        6M-10M-12M horns. They incorporate design features of
        the M Series instruments, and are very sought after for th
        well built instruments.
M Series
        Conn started making the M Series instruments in the late
        were several years when transitionals and M Series horns
        by side. They are characterized by the 6M alto's tuning so
```

Figure 23.A Definition list is made up of Term- and Definition-formatted paragraphs.

Figure 24. After you enter a term, the next line automatically indents for the definition.

Creating Definition Lists

Definition Lists use alternating indents to differentiate terms and their definitions, as in a glossary (**Figure 23**). They're made up of two paragraph formats: Term and Definition.

To create a definition list:

1. Place the cursor where you want to enter the definition list, then choose Definition List from the Format menu and Term from the submenu.

2. Type in the first term, then press Enter (Windows) or Return (Mac) to move to the next line.

    The paragraph style automatically changes to Definition and the insertion point is indented, showing you where the text you enter will start (**Figure 24**).

3. Enter the definition of the first term, then press Enter (Windows) or Return (Mac).

    The insertion point advances another line, and the style changes back to Term. The Term and Definition formats continue to alternate in this fashion.

4. Repeat steps 2 and 3 until your list is complete.

✔ Tip

■ To format a list you've already typed in, you have to apply the Term and Definition paragraph styles one by one.

Changing Text Alignment

Paragraph alignment works just like it does in a word processing application. You can align any paragraph in one of three ways: Left (flush left, ragged right), Right (flush right, ragged left), or Centered (**Figure 25**).

To align a paragraph:

1. Place the insertion point anywhere in the paragraph you want to align.

2. Choose Alignment from the Format menu and choose one of the alignment options (**Figure 26**).

or

Click one of the Alignment buttons on the Styles toolbar.

✔ Tips

■ All alignments are with respect to the browser window. HTML has no provision for justified (both margins flush) text.

■ The default setting for text is Aligned Left.

Alignment buttons

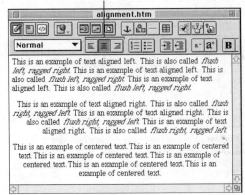

Figure 25. You can align paragraphs in any one of the three ways above using HTML formatting.

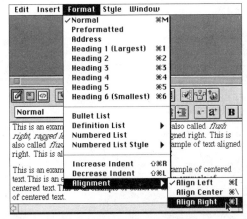

Figure 26. The Alignment submenu shows the keyboard shortcuts for aligning left, center, and right.

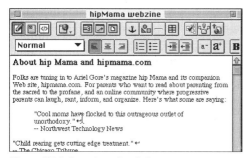

Figure 27. Indentation is handy for quotes.

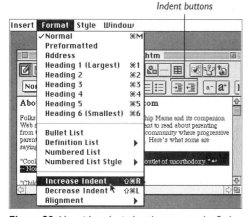

Figure 28. Use either the indent buttons on the Styles toolbar or the indent items in the Format menu to change the indentation of a selected paragraph.

Using Paragraph Indentation

Indenting offsets text for a specific purpose, to set apart a quote from the body of your text for example (**Figure 27**).

To increase or decrease paragraph indentation:

1. Place the insertion point anywhere in the paragraph you want to indent.

2. Choose Increase Indent or Decrease Indent from the Format menu (**Figure 28**).

   or

   Click the increase or decrease indent button on the Styles toolbar.

✔ Tip

■ HTML sets paragraphs apart with an extra space, so you can't indent just the first line unless you use the preformatted style.

Good Web Practice

A word of warning.

Before we get into text formatting, a word of warning is in order. The World Wide Web has a feature that has rankled many a print designer (including this one). Despite your best efforts to make your pages look just so, the *client* system, on the receiving end, determines much of a page's look. This is especially true of text. If the client is set up to display all text in the font Spumoni, point size 24, that's how the end user views your pages. To complicate matters further, different browsers handle text differently, as do different platforms.

If your company logo happens to be in Times, somewhere on the World Wide Web someone will view it in Spumoni. If there is text you absolutely must have right, you'll need to make it an image file. We'll cover this in the next chapter.

About Character Formatting

Like paragraph styles, character styles control font size and style, but they're applied to individually selected text instead of to entire paragraphs (**Figure 29**).

Character formatting consists of physical and logical styles. The difference between them lies in the way browsers interpret them.

Physical Styles

Physical styles are familiar from word processing: bold, italic, underlined, and so on (**Figure 30**). All browsers that support physical styles will display them in the same way, so you have much more text control with these styles.

To apply a physical style:

1. Select the word or text block you want to format using one of the methods described in Chapter 1.

2. Choose one of the physical styles from the Style menu (**Figure 31**).

   or

   If you're formatting italic or bold, click the corresponding button on the Styles toolbar.

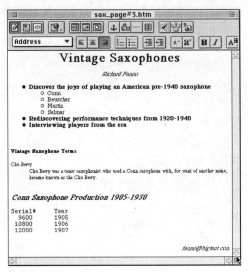

Figure 29. This document uses a combination of paragraph and character Styles.

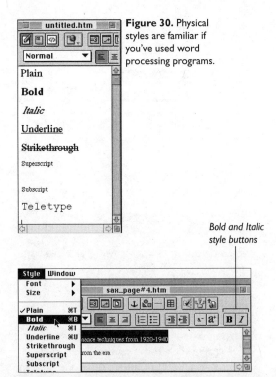

Figure 30. Physical styles are familiar if you've used word processing programs.

Bold and Italic style buttons

Figure 31. You can style text Bold and Italic from the Style toolbar or by using their keyboard shortcuts.

Figure 32. Logical styles appearance depends on viewer browser configuration.

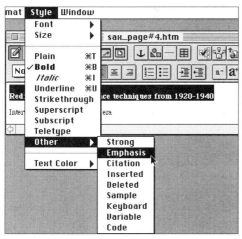

Figure 33. Choose one of the logical styles from the Other menu in the Style menu...if you dare.

Logical Styles

Logical styles came along with HTML and have less familiar distinctions: Strong, Emphasis, Code, and so on (**Figure 32**).These styles appear differently depending on browser configuration, so the person who controls the browser preferences file has most of the control over how these styles display. For example, in one browser Emphasis might display in italics and as underlined in another. Logical styles are also used less and less these days because many of them look like physical styles, and because they afford you little control over how your page looks on a browser.

To apply a logical style:

1. Select the word or text block you want to format.

2. Choose Other from the Style menu, then choose one of the Logical styles from the resulting submenu (**Figure 33**).

✔ Tip

■ You can apply both physical and logical styles to the same text. For example, if you apply Bold to a word already formatted with Emphasis, the viewer will most likely see a bold, italicized word.

Coloring Text

You can change the color of any text in Claris Home Page. You assign colors using Character Styles, which override the default text color settings on your page.

To change the color of selected text:

1. Select the text you wish to change.

2. Select Text Color from the Style Menu (**Figure 34**),

   or

   Click the Text Color button on the Styles toolbar (Figure 35).

3. Choose one of the predefined colors from either one of these color lists, or choose Other to open the Color dialog box and experiment with other color options.

✔ Tip

■ Color on the World Wide Web is a very delicate issue, an area for only the most intrepid. Because receiving systems often cannot duplicate the colors as you want them to appear, you're usually better off using the colors in the predefined color palette, which are known to reproduce well on most systems.

To return text to the default color:

1. Select the text you wish to return to the default color.

2. Choose Text Color from the Style menu, then choose Default.

   or

   Choose default from the text color button drop-down list.

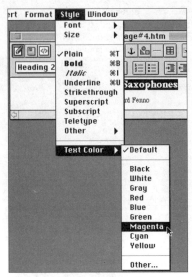

Figure 34. You can choose color from the Style menu...

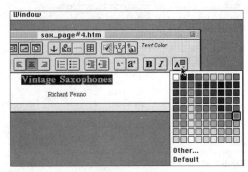

Figure 35. ...or from Styles toolbar.

GRAPHICS
AND MULTIMEDIA

Figure 1. Your Web page will start jumping…

…with graphics like animated GIFs.

The Web was once a text-based medium—a useful if dull tool, linking scientists and their research to the rest of the world. Then two graphics formats—GIF and JPEG—transformed the World Wide Web into an exciting visual medium. Graphics and multimedia make the Web the irresistible place it is, and point to the exciting, unexplored territory it will become.

With Home Page, you can easily add colorful design elements and backgrounds, digitized photographs, and image-based features such as buttons and menu bars, and image maps to your Web pages. You can also enliven your page with multimedia files: audio, animation, and even video.

Images: Make 'em or Take 'em

If you make your own images, remember that there are only two acceptable formats in use on the Web today, GIF and JPEG. Don't worry if you can't save in these formats with your graphics program, Home Page automatically converts images to one of the Web-friendly formats as long as you save your images as PICT or BMP files (**Figure 2**). Most graphics programs for the Mac can save files in PICT format, and most programs for Windows can save files in BMP format.

If you don't have an artistic bent (although that's not enough to stop a lot of folks), Home Page provides a vast collection of backgrounds, buttons, animated GIFs, and other design art to enliven your site. They're all available through libraries placed on your hard drive during installation (see Chapter 6 to learn how to use libraries).

✔ Tip

■ To set a default folder where Home Page will store all your images, choose Application Options from the Tools menu (Windows) or Preferences from the Edit menu (Mac). Click the Images tab and select a folder under Convert and Save Automatically to Directory (Windows) or Convert and Save Automatically to Folder (Mac) (**Figure 3**).

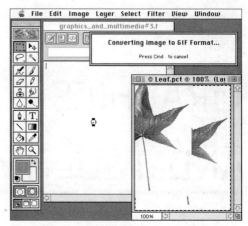

Figure 2. Home Page displays this small dialog box for only a moment, telling you it's working on converting your images to a Web-friendly format.

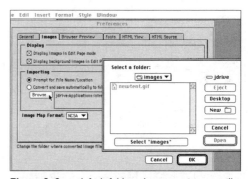

Figure 3. Set a default folder where your images will be saved so they'll be easy to find and work with.

Good Web Practice

Making Your Own Images

If you're building your own art, use a resolution of 72 dots per inch. You're building screen images here, not files for high-resolution printing. Smaller files make for quicker downloads and make your site a more pleasant place to visit. Learn how to cut down on colors to keep file sizes small.

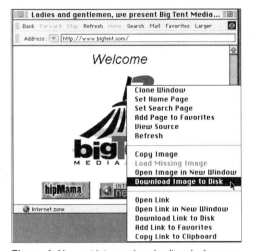

Figure 4. Along with image downloading, the browser pop-up menu offers a number of features such as cloning a window, viewing HTML source code, and adding the page to your bookmark, or favorites, list.

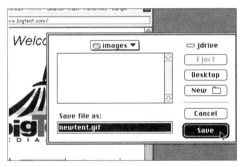

Figure 5. Save the image with the name it has, or rename it in the Save file as text field, and put it directly into your images folder to start off on the right foot with file management.

To download an image from another Web site:

1. With your browser open and while you're connected to the Web, click and hold (Mac) or right click (Windows) on the image you wish to copy.

2. Choose Download Image to Disk (Explorer) or Save This Image As (Navigator) from the pop-up menu (**Figure 4**). A dialog box asks where you want to put the copied file.

3. Select the images folder you created in your site folder (**Figure 5**).

✔ Tips

- **Important:** If you download an image from someone else's page, be sure you're not stealing anyone's copyrighted property. When in doubt, always ask for clearance to use an image, and get agreements in writing.

- You can also copy an image location using the browser pop-up menus. This method lets you tell your Web page to load the image from someone else's server. However, you sacrifice page loading speed and control over whether the image is even maintained on the external server, so this method is best avoided.

- If you want to use a company logo or a bit of art, check with the graphic artist who created it to see if there's a file you can use. Don't forget to describe the approximate size you will need. It's usually easier for the image's creator to make that adjustment on the other end.

- America Online won't support numerals in file names, so if AOL is your server, don't use them.

Downloading Images from a Web Site

GIF and JPEG Formats

Compuserve Information Service developed the GIF format just for the Web, and **GIF** is now the file format of choice for displaying nonphotographic images online. Its 256-color limit is ideal for simple images (**Figure 6**). GIF files are tightly compressed, and display equally well on most platforms.

GIF format also allows transparency and interlacing (which you'll learn about later in this chapter), and can display a simple sequence of images for animation effects.

JPEG, or more accurately JPEG/JFIF, is a standard compression method the Joint Photographic Experts Group adopted to display more complex color palettes. JPEGs can display millions of colors (**Figure 7**). JPEG files are usually photographic images converted from TIFF format by an image editor such as Photoshop.

JPEG can't show transparent areas as GIF can, nor can it animate a series of images. However, newer browsers can display Progressive JPEG files, which like interlaced GIFs display a rough image while the complete JPEG file loads. For more information on Progressive JPEGs, look on the Home Page Visual Quickstart Guide Web site, http://www.bigtent.com/chp3.

✔ Tip

- If JPEG images do not display correctly in Home Page but look fine in a browser, you need to check the application configuration. In Windows, a file called accuisr5.dll must be installed in the same directory as Home Page. Mac users should make sure they have QuickTime version 2.0 or higher installed in the Extensions folder.

Figure 6. This image is simple and GIF-worthy...

Figure 7. ...whereas this image needs the subtlety of JPEG's expanded color options.

Good Web Practice

Use JPEG wisely.

JPEG can compress a file's color information so much that image quality is compromised. The real trick to using JPEG is to compress a file as much as possible without crossing the line where the eye can see color loss.

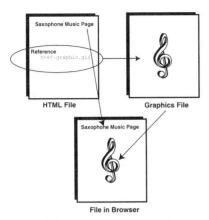

Figure 8. Images and HTML source files are stored separately and combined by the viewer's browser.

Figure 9. Use the Insert menu to insert an image...

Figure 10. ...or click the Insert Image button.

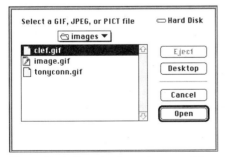

Figure 11. You'll need to know the name of the image file you want in order to place it using the Select a GIF dialog box.

Adding Images to Your Page

Adding images to a page actually means adding an HTML *reference* to the *location* of an image file (along with some information that tells Web browsers how to display it) to the HTML code that makes up your page.

When a browser loads a page, the HTML and the images are loaded separately. Then the browser assembles them all into a completed page (**Figure 8**).

To place an image on your page:

1. Place the insertion point where you want the image to appear on your page.

2. Choose Image from the Insert menu (**Figure 9**), or click the Insert Image button on the Styles toolbar (**Figure 10**).

3. A dialog box appears (**Figure 11**). Select the image file and click Open.

Good Web Practice
Organization first!

Nothing ruins a visit to a Web site like the broken-link icon, which usually represents an image the server can't find. You'll learn more about keeping your files organized in Chapter 9, but for now, remember these simple rules:

• Keep all your HTML files in a site folder.

• Keep all your images and other media files in a well-named folders inside this site folder.

To drag and drop an image onto your page:

1. Select the image you want to place from an open document, or select its icon on your hard drive (**Figure 12**).

2. Click and drag the icon or image onto the open Home Page file window (**Figure 13**).

3. Release the mouse button (**Figure 14**).

To cut and paste or copy and paste an image onto your page:

1. Select the image you want to use on your Web page (**Figure 15**). This image can be in another Home Page document, or any other application.

2. Choose Cut or Copy from the Edit menu.

3. Place the insertion point where you wish the image to appear on your page.

4. Choose Paste from the Edit menu. You will be asked to name the file and place it in the default folder for converted images. Once you name it, the image appears in position on the page (**Figure 16**).

Figure 12. You don't have to have an image open to drag and drop it; dragging its icon will do the trick.

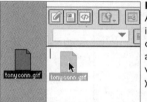

Figure 13. A shadow of the icon (or a silhouette of the image) appears on the page where you'll drop your image.

Figure 14. Drop the icon onto the page. Home Page stores it in the folder you specified in your Preferences and, if necessary, automatically converts it into a Web-friendly GIF format.

Good Web Practice

What's in a name?

Web servers can be finicky about naming conventions, so you should be, too. To make GIF files easy to find, I always name them with lowercase letters and make sure the files end with a .gif extension.

Figure 15. In a graphics application or another Home Page document, select the image you want and use Copy or Cut to place it in the clipboard.

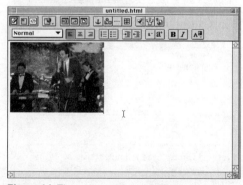

Figure 16. Then paste it into your document.

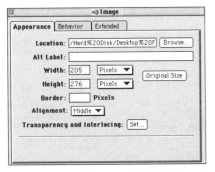

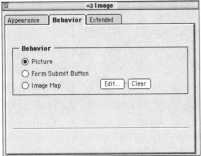

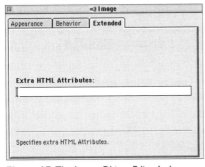

Figure 17. The Image Object Editor's three tabs have a number of different settings to work with.

Opening the Image Object Editor

Once an image is on the page, you can change its properties with the Image Object Editor. The Object Editor makes it easy to optimize and customize image files so your pages load faster and display exactly how you want them to.

To open the Image Object Editor:

While in Edit mode, double-click an image on your page.

or

Select the image and click the Object Editor button on the toolbar.

The Object Editor appears (**Figure 17**).

There are three tabs in the Object Editor: Appearance, Behavior, and Extended. The Appearance tab controls the most important options for this chapter: setting interlacing and transparency on GIF files, setting alternate text labels for an image, resizing an image, setting borders around images, and aligning images on the page.

Figure 18. A broken link icon appears when an image file cannot be found.

Good Web Practice

Use a text label for every image.

Ideally, every image should have a text label associated with it.

Attaching a label to each image (GIF or JPEG) is useful for the folks out there still using text-only browsers, for browsers with image loading intentionally disabled, or for identifying problems

with missing files. When the image does not load, the missing file icon and the text label appear instead (**Figure 18**). To add a text label to an image, open the Image Object Editor and fill in a descriptive text label for the image in the Alt Label field, then close the Image Object Editor to save the text label.

Sizing an Image

It's always a good idea to size your images in a graphics application to achieve maximum resolution quality and image size control, but that's not always possible. You can change size in Home Page, but keep in mind that a small version of a large file takes just as long to load as the original file.

To resize an image:

1. Open the Image Object Editor by double-clicking the image. Make sure the Appearance tab is selected.

2. Enter the new image size, measured either in pixels or as a percent (**Figure 19**),

   or

   Select the handle on the lower right corner of the image, hold down the shift key, and click and and drag the image. You can try zany effects by pulling the picture's handles without regard to keeping the image proportional (**Figure 20**).

3. To return an image to its original size and proportions, click the Original Size button (**Figure 21**) in the Image Object Editor, or double-click the bottom right handle of the image.

   Double-clicking the right handle returns the image to its original width, double-clicking the bottom handle returns the image to its original height.

Figure 19. You can size an image with absolute width and heights, or as a percentage of its original size.

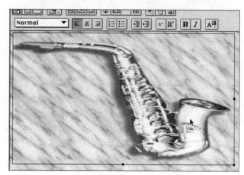

Figure 20. Pull the resizing handles without regard to proportion for wild effects.

Figure 21. You can always go back to the original image size by clicking the Original size button.

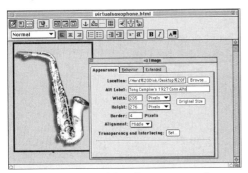

Figure 22. A border of 4 pixels as it appears after entering the Border setting in the Image Editor.

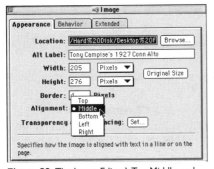

Figure 23. The Image Editor's Top, Middle, and Bottom Alignment settings determine the position of text adjacent to an image.

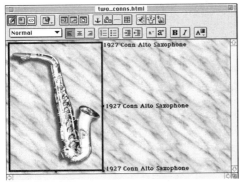

Figure 24. Composite image showing the three vertical alignment options.

Adding Image Borders

You can add a border to any image on a page.

To set a border around an image:

1. Double-click the image.

2. In the Object Editor, set the border width (in pixels) by entering a number between 1 and 100 in the Border dialog box. Press the (Enter) (Windows), or (Return) (Mac) to see what the border looks like (**Figure 22**).

✔ Tip

- While border widths for various images can differ, their colors will be the same, as determined by your preference setting.

Aligning Images

You can align images on a page in two different ways: *vertically*, to control the relationship of the text and the image, and *horizontally*, to control the object's position on the Web page itself.

To align text and an image vertically:

1. Double-click the image to open the Image Object Editor.

2. Choose Top, Middle, or Bottom from the drop-down Alignment menu (**Figure 23**).

   The surrounding text aligns to the top, middle, or bottom of the image (**Figure 24**).

To align an image horizontally:

Select the image and click Align Left, Align Center, or Align Right on the Styles Toolbar,

or

Choose Alignment from the Format menu and choose one of the submenu options,

or

Open the Image Object Editor and choose Left or Right from the alignment drop-down menu. (You cannot center images horizontally from this menu.)

ADDING IMAGE BORDERS ■ ALIGNING IMAGES

Interlacing GIF Files

One of the virtues of GIF files is that you can *interlace* them. This means that when a browser loads the image, a rough version quickly appears so viewers can get an idea of what they're waiting for (**Figure 25**). The details fill in as the download continues (**Figure 26**).

Home Page can convert any GIF file into an interlaced GIF.

To Interlace a GIF file:

1. Double-click a GIF file to open the Image Object Editor. Make sure the Appearance tab is selected.

2. Click the Set button (**Figure 27**) at the bottom of the Object Editor. The Transparency and Interlacing Image Editor opens.

3. Click the Interlace button on the toolbar (**Figure 28**). The selected GIF file is now interlaced and loads a low-resolution version before filling in the entire, higher-resolution file. To return the file to a non-interlaced format, click the Don't Interlace button on the toolbar.

4. Close the Transparency and Interlacing Image Editor, and make the changes permanent by clicking Save when prompted.

✔ Tip

■ You can opt to make your GIF images interlaced by default. Select the make Interlaced GIFs check box in the Images section of the Preferences menu (**Figure 29**).

Figure 25. Rough versions of interlaced GIF files load quickly, with large, square pixels.

Figure 26. The finished, detailed version of the interlaced GIF files takes just a few seconds to load.

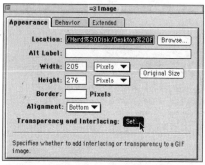

Figure 27. Click the Set button to open the Transparency and Interlacing Image Editor.

Interlace
Don't interlace

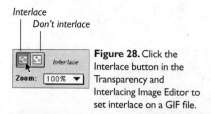

Figure 28. Click the Interlace button in the Transparency and Interlacing Image Editor to set interlace on a GIF file.

Figure 29. Selecting Make Interlaced GIFs will make all files converted by Home Page into interlaced GIFs. Check this box in the Preferences or Application Options menu, under the Images tab.

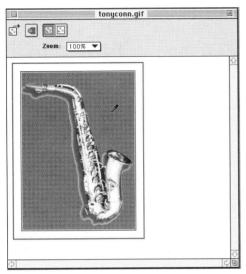

Figure 30. Transparency and Interlacing for GIF files are set here in the Transparency and Interlacing Image Editor.

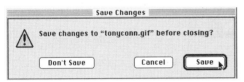

Figure 31. When transparency is set, save the changes to the file by clicking the close button and then Save in this dialog box.

Making Transparent GIF Files

Transparent GIF files make one color in an image transparent. This enables you to do things such as make the background of your Web page show through and image.

To set transparency in a GIF file:

1. Double-click the image4 to open the Object Editor. Make sure the Appearance tab is selected.

2. Click the Set button at the bottom of the editor. The Transparency and Interlacing Image Editor opens (**Figure 30**). The cursor becomes an eyedropper when you drag it across the image.

3. Place the eyedropper over the color you want to make transparent and click. This color becomes transparent throughout the image.

4. Close the Transparency and Interlacing Image Editor and make the changes permanent by clicking Save when you are prompted (**Figure 31**).

✔ Tip

■ You can open the Transparency and Interlacing Image Editor directly by right-clicking the GIF file (Windows) or holding down the option key and double-clicking an image (Mac).

Background Color and Patterns

On the Web, default gray is the equivalent of a student apartment's white walls. That may be fine for some, but you can select from a wide array of page backgrounds. Your backgrounds can be either a solid color or a GIF or JPEG image. If you choose an image, it can be either full-page or tiled to fill the entire page.

To set the background color:

1. Choose Document Options from the Tools menu (Windows) or the Edit menu (Mac) or click the Document Options button on the Styles toolbar. The Document Options dialog box appears.

2. Click and hold the Color button. A drop-down color palette appears (**Figure 32**).

3. Select one of the colors in the palette. If none of the preset palette colors suits your tastes, choose Other at the bottom of the palette window. This opens your system's color picker (**Figure 33**), which you can use to set a customized color.

4. Click OK to close the dialog box and return to your page, which now has your selected color as its background.

✔ Tips

■ Just because a color looks good on your screen doesn't mean it will reproduce accurately when viewed in a browser. It's best for newcomers to stick with one of the color palettes Home Page provides. Choose Preferences from the Tools menu (Windows) or Edit menu (Mac), select the General tab, and choose a palette from the Color Palette dialog box.

■ To return to the default background, click the Restore Default Background button in the Document Options dialog box.

■ To remove a background image you've set, click the Remove button in the Document Options dialog box.

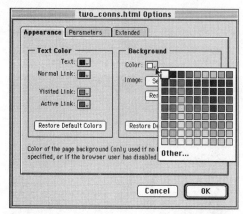

Figure 32. You can choose from any of the palette colors, load a different palette, or choose Other to go to your computer's color picker for more choices.

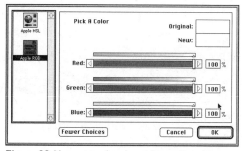

Figure 33. Your system's color picker options let you choose customized colors.

Good Web Practice

Use caution when picking your colors.

Let good design sense prevail. A background color or image should never conflict with text elements. Some background colors are so bright they can inflict headaches on people visiting your site. Generally speaking, if it obscures the meaning or readability of your text, don't use it.

BACKGROUND COLOR AND PATTERNS

Figure 34. Take advantage of contrast differences when placing text against a large GIF or JPEG background.

Figure 35. This marbled effect is made up of many small, smooth images tiled to create a continuous look.

Set button   Thumbnail

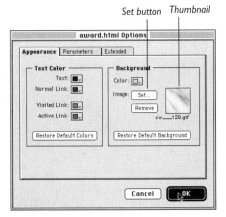

Figure 36. The background image you've selected is displayed as a small thumbnail.

Using Background Images

Backgrounds open up many design possibilities. For example, you can use GIF and JPEG image files as backgrounds, adding a pictorial dimension to your page. A large background image can fill an entire page (**Figure 34**) while smaller files automatically tile, that is, they repeat to fill the whole page (**Figure 35**).

To use an image as a background:

1. Select a file to use as a background image. Although you can use a full-screen image (usually 640 by 480 pixels), most backgrounds are made up of smaller "tiles."

2. Click the Document Options button on the Styles Toolbar or choose Document Options from the Tools (Windows) or Edit menu (Mac) to open the Document Options dialog box.

3. With the Appearance tab selected, click the Set button in the Background section of the dialog box.

4. Locate the image file you want to use in the Select an Image File menu and click Open.

   A thumbnail of the background image appears in the preview window of the Document Options dialog box (**Figure 36**), with the file location of the image file indicated below.

5. Click OK to close the Document Options dialog box. Your page now displays the new background.

To turn off your background while working:

1. Choose Preferences from the Application Options (Windows) or Edit menu (Mac). Click the Images tab and deselect the Display Background Images in Edit Mode check box (**Figure 37**).

   This way, your page doesn't take as long to redraw.

✔ Tips

■ If you have selected a color for a background and then select an image, the image prevails. The color will not appear on the page unless you remove the image background by clicking the Remove button in the Background dialog box.

■ Background images should go inside the images folder within the site folder.

■ Look in the Content folder (which is inside the Home Page folder) for a folder called Backgrounds. It contains a terrific assortment of background files that you can experiment with.

Figure 37. If your system is pokey, try turning off the display of background images in Edit mode.

Figure 38. Netscape's plug-in page gives an idea of what's happening in Internet multimedia.

Figure 39. When you start accumulating a lot of files, a little organization can be a big help.

Multimedia File Management

Multimedia enhances Web pages with sound, animation, and video. Browsers use small, free applications called plug-ins to view most multimedia files (**Figure 38**). Viewers must have the plug-ins installed to view your multimedia files. If they don't, Home Page automatically directs them to a Web site where they can download the necessary free files.

The most popular plug-in technologies are

◆ QuickTime and QuickTime VR, used for everything from movies to music and sound files to 3-D virtual reality.

◆ **Java,** which produces applets for a number of purposes, including images that perform various tricks, animation, and to program pages to go beyond what HTML can do on its own.

◆ **Shockwave,** from Macromedia, which compresses images, animation, and sound using special applications so Web sites can use them.

For more information about Java, Shockwave, and other products, go to the Home Page companion Web site: http://www.bigtent.com/chp3.

✔ Tip

■ Keep in mind that some of these programs may affect download times.

Adding multimedia is a lot like adding images, that reference files and their locations, rather than the files themselves. As with images, you should tuck your multimedia files into a special folder within your site folder (call the new folder media or some other title that you'll remember) (**Figure 39**).

MULTIMEDIA FILE MANAGEMENT

Adding Multimedia Files

The basic procedure for adding all multimedia files is the same: you create the multimedia file, place it in your media folder, insert it on your page and customize behavior options, and test the multimedia in Browser mode.

We'll use the case of inserting a QuickTime movie as an example. QuickTime is a useful cross-platform standard that can handle both audio and video in one fell swoop.

To add a QuickTime movie to your Web page:

1. Place the insertion point on your page where you want the movie to appear.

2. Choose QuickTime Movie from the Insert menu (**Figure 40**).

3. When the Select a QuickTime Movie dialog box opens, select a QuickTime movie (**Figure 41**). If you don't have your own, navigate to the movie folder in the content folder, which is in the Claris Home Page application folder.

4. The first frame of your QuickTime movie (or an icon, if it's not a movie file) appears at the insertion point on the page (**Figure 42**).

✔ Tips

■ You can see or hear a QuickTime movie only in Browser mode.

■ QuickTime files are generally called movies, even when they contain just audio. All QuickTime files must have the file extensions .mov or .snm to run in a Web browser. Home Page installs several of these files in its content folder for you to experiment with.

Figure 40. Use the menu to place your QuickTime movie.

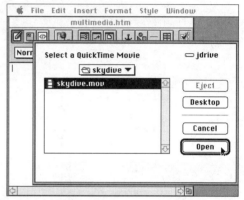

Figure 41. Home Page comes with a couple of QuickTime movies for you to play with.

Figure 42. The first frame of the QuickTime video appears at the insertion point. QuickTime videos can be viewed only in Preview in Browser mode.

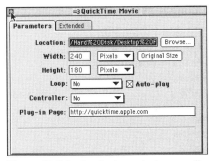

Figure 43. Selecting the Auto-play button will make the movie play automatically when the movie file is downloaded.

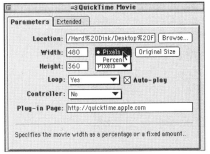

Figure 44. When you resize a QuickTime movie's container box, the movie does not change size; only the box containing it changes.

Figure 45. Use the sizing handles of the selected QuickTime movie to resize the container box of the movie.

To set play options with the QuickTime Object Editor:

1. Double-click the movie frame to open the QuickTime Object Editor,

   or

   Choose Object Editor from the View menu (Windows) or Show Object Editor from the Window menu (Mac).

2. In the Parameters tab, you can set the following Play options for your movie:

   ♦ To make the movie start playing automatically when the page is downloaded, choose No from the Loop drop-down menu and select the Auto-play check box (Figure 43).

   ♦ To have the movie play continuously once it's loaded, choose Yes from the Loop drop-down menu and select the Auto-play check box.

   ♦ If you want the movie to play forward until it reaches the end, then play backward, then forward again, and so on, select Auto-Reverse from the Loop drop-down menu and select the Auto-play check box.

To resize a QuickTime movie:

1. Double-click the movie frame to open the QuickTime Object Editor,

   or

   Choose Object Editor from the View menu (Windows) or Show Object Editor from the Window menu (Mac).

2. Enter a new width and height in pixels or as a percent of the browser's height and width (**Figure 44**). To return the movie to its original size, click the Original Size button in the Parameters tab window. Close the Object Editor to see the changes. You can also manipulate the size of the movie by dragging the box handles in Edit mode (**Figure 45**).

To add a controller bar to a movie:

1. Double-click the movie frame to open the QuickTime Object Editor,

   or

   Choose Object Editor from the View menu (Windows) or Show Object Editor from the Window menu (Mac).

2. Select Yes in the Controller drop-down menu (**Figure 46**). The controller bar allows the viewer to start, stop, and pause the movie (**Figure 47**).

   Selecting No removes the Controller, giving the user no control over the playing of the movie.

The last item in the QuickTime Movie Object Editor, the Plug-in Page box, shows the Web location where users can download the QuickTime extensions and plug-ins (**Figure 46**) they don't have. Only change this Web address if you know of a better place than Home Page suggests for plug-in downloads.

To view your movie:

1. When you have adjusted all your QuickTime movie play options, close the Object Editor.

2. Go to View in Browser mode and test the QuickTime movie (**Figure 48**).

Plug-in download URL

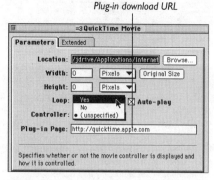

Figure 46. You can set the controller option and location of necessary plug-ins needed to view your QuickTime movies in the Parameters tab.

Controller

Figure 47. The controller bar allows the visitor to control the playing of the QuickTime movie on the receiving end.

Figure 48. QuickTime movies can be viewed and tested in Preview in Browser mode. In this case, the movie will be started by clicking the start (left) button on the control bar.

LINKS AND ANCHORS

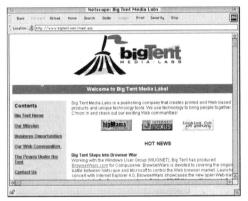

Figure 1. This publishing company's main page includes text links to pages within the site, and text and graphical links to external sites.

The World Wide Web has grown as quickly as it has in part because it allows users to jump from one place to another very easily. This is the Web's most compelling feature. At times it seems the Web lets you skip across the pond of human knowledge, clicking from one site to the next, navigating hyperdimensionally through a single site, or going to specific locations within a page.

The link is the basic tool that makes this inter-activity possible. Links let the user branch out from one site to another, directly to an e-mail composition window, or to another Web service like Usenet or an FTP download-ing page.

Any text or image on your page can act as a starting point, or the source link, that con-nects to any *destination* within your site or out on the Web.

In this chapter you will learn to make three kinds of links:

♦ *Text links,* which are clickable characters, words, or text blocks that lead users to new destinations

♦ *Graphic links,* which use an image as a jumping-off point

♦ *Image maps,* which are graphic images that contain multiple clickable *hot spots,* each jumping to a different destination

About URLs

URL stands for Universal Resource Locator. A URL is the precise address or location used to access Web sites and pages. Before starting to link pages, there are two types of URLs you need to know about:

♦ *Absolute* URLs reference external pages and contain all of the Web address information from http:// onward. For example, creating a link to http://www.peachpit.com takes you to the Peachpit Press Web site.

♦ *Relative* URLs reference documents within a site and include the directory pathway that leads to it. You use these URLs to jump from one page to another within your site. For example, MySite/people/friends/igor.html takes you to the HTML page honoring your friend Igor, which is in the friends directory inside the people directory of MySite.

Introducing the Link Editor

Home Page's Link Editor simplifies linking content. The Link Editor uses a simple URL window and gives examples of how to phrase your references.

To open the Link Editor:

1. Open a file and click the Link Editor button on the toolbar. The Link Editor appears (**Figure 2**).

2. Click Show Examples. The Link Editor expands (**Figure 3**), offering a good look at the different things you can link to.
   Table 1 explains these options.

✔ Tip

■ The bottom half of the Link Editor dialog box provides a menu for setting up links to frame sets. You'll learn about frame sets in Chapter 8.

Link Editor button

Figure 2. One way to create your links is by entering the URL you want to link to in the URL text field. The URL above points to a page and to an anchor on that page, referenced by the #conn in the address.

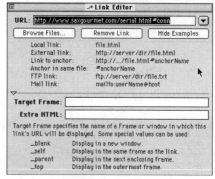

Figure 3. Clicking Show Examples reveals a list of the various links you can create.

Table I. The different types of links

TYPE OF LINK	WHAT IT DOES
Local	Links to another file on your system.
External	Links to a file on another Web site.
Anchor	Links to a fixed place in another file.
Anchor in same file	Links to a specific place in the same file.
FTP	Links to an FTP site.
Mail	Links to an e-mail address.

Figure 4. Clicking the Browse Files button in the Link Editor allows you to scan the files on your system to find the one you want to link to.

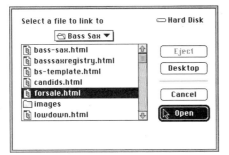

Figure 5. You can navigate to any HTML file in your hard drive using the Select a file to link to dialog box.

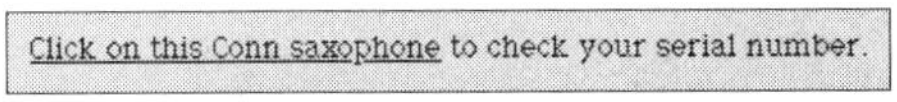

Click on this Conn saxophone to check your serial number.

Figure 6. Linked text is underlined, indicating that clicking it will send a user to another destination either on your site or out on the Web somewhere.

Good Web Practice

Storyboarding

Sit down with a pencil and paper before you write your Web pages. A small amount of planning will make your programming time much more effective.

♦ Create a diagram of the links that connect your pages or lead to other Web sites.

♦ Make sure that all related pages are linked and that they all link back to a main page.

♦ Define the external links you want to use.

Linking Your Pages Together

In linking pages together, you will either refer to a *local* file, one within your own site, or an *external* file, one that is out on the Web.

To create a text link to another page within your site:

1. Open a Home Page document and highlight the text you wish to make into a link.

2. Click the Link Editor button on the toolbar, then click the Browse Files button (**Figure 4**). Select the file you want to link to from the dialog box, and click Open (**Figure 5**).

   or

   Choose Link to File from the Insert menu, select the file you want to link to from the list and click Open.

3. Close the Link Editor.

   The selected text is now underlined and blue, indicating a link (**Figure 6**).

4. Test your link in Preview mode by clicking the underlined blue text. The linked page opens in its own window.

To create an image link to another page within your site:

1. Place an image on your page.

2. Select the image by clicking it once.

3. Click the Link Editor button on the toolbar, then select the Browse Files button. Select the file you want to link to from the dialog box, and click Open.

   or

   Choose Link to File from the Insert menu (**Figure 7**), select the file you want to link to from the list, and click Open.

4. Close the Link Editor.

   The image now has a blue border, indicating a link (**Figure 8**).

5. Test your link in Preview mode by clicking the underlined blue text. The linked page opens in its own window.

To hide the image link border:

1. Double-click the linked image you want to change to open the Image Object Editor.

2. Enter the number 0 in the Border Field (**Figure 9**). The link will still function but the border will be invisible.

To remove a link:

1. Select the linked text or image and click the Link Editor button.

2. Click Remove Link (**Figure 10**).

✔ Tip

■ In Preview mode, a small icon at the bottom of the page helps you keep track of where your links lead to (**Figure 11**).

Figure 7. Use this menu option, or click the Link Editor button to open your Link Editor.

Figure 8. The blue border around the image indicates that it is a live link.

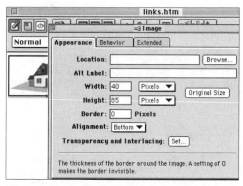

Figure 9. To remove the blue border from a linked graphic, open the Image Object Editor and change the pixel border value to 0.

Figure 10. Just highlight a link and click the Remove Link button to unlink text or graphics.

Figure 11. Place your cursor over a link to see where it leads.

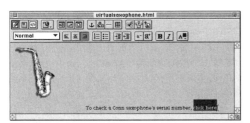

Figure 12. Create links that describe where the user will be going.

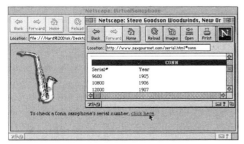

Figure 13. By default, Home Page opens a new window for the linked site. This is so that folks won't drift off into the nether regions of the Web and forget where they started—at your page!

Figure 14. The Link Editor gives you access to two lists of URLs. The first is made up of recently used URLs. The feature is useful if you are linking to a fixed group of files a number of times in your site.

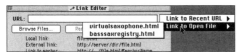

Figure 15. The second list shows files that are currently open in Home Page.

Linking to Another Web Site

As long as you can find another site on the Web, you can find its URL in the location field of your browser. And if you know its URL, you can link to it. You can set up any text block or image as a link that sends your visitors from your site to another Web site with the click of a mouse button.

To create a text link to an external Web site:

1. Select the text you want to use as a link (**Figure 12**) and click the Link Editor button on the toolbar.

   or

   Choose Link to URL from the Insert menu. The Link Editor opens.

2. Enter the URL of the page you wish to link to in the URL field.

3. Close the Link Editor.

4. The text is now underlined, indicating the link has been created.

5. Test the link by going to Browser mode, connecting to the Web, and clicking on the link (**Figure 13**).

✔ Tips

- To ensure accuracy in your links, open the page you wish to link to in your browser, copy the URL from the browser location field, and paste it into the Link Editor URL field.

- Click the button to the right of the URL window to link to recently used URLs (**Figure 14**) or to link to an open Claris Home Page file (**Figure 15**). These two lists can be real timesavers.

To link an image to an external Web site:

1. Select the image you want to use as a link (**Figure 16**) by clicking it once, and click the Link Editor button on the toolbar.
   or
   Choose Link to URL from the Insert menu. The Link Editor opens.

2. Enter the URL of the page you wish to link to in the URL field (**Figure 17**).

3. Close the Link Editor.

4. The image is now outlined (**Figure 18**), indicating that your link is established.

5. Test the link by going to Browser mode, connecting to the Web, and clicking the image.

To hide the image link border:

1. Double-click the linked image to open the Image Object Editor.

2. Enter the number 0 in the Border Field. The image link will still function, but the blue border will be invisible.

✔ Tip

■ Some users browse pages with graphics turned off. For this reason, it is a good idea to include text links along with image links on your pages (**Figure 19**).

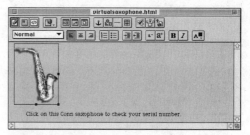

Figure 16. To make a link with a graphic, first select the graphic image by clicking it.

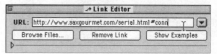

Figure 17. It's best to paste in the URL of the page you want to link to in the URL window.

Figure 18. A blue border around an image tells you it's a link. You can keep this indicator on your page or remove the border.

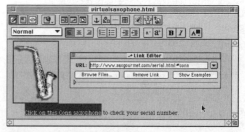

Figure 19. Both the picture of the saxophone and the underlined text are linked to the same place, providing the visitor multiple options.

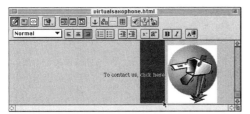

Figure 20. This text is selected and will be used to make an e-mail link.

Figure 21. Using the syntax in the Link Editor, fill in the mail address. The method is the same on a text link or a graphic image.

Figure 22. The graphic has a blue line around it, and the text is underlined, indicating they are both links.

Figure 23. Linking to an e-mail address automatically opens an e-mail composition window.

Linking to an E-mail Address

One simple form of interactivity you can add to your Web pages is the ability for users to send you feedback via e-mail. Whether it's an item you're offering for sale, an idea you express, or a typo you've made, your readers will want to respond!

1. Select the text or image you want to link to an e-mail address (**Figure 20**), then click the Link Editor button on the toolbar.

   or

   Choose Link to URL from the Insert menu. The Link Editor opens.

2. Click Show Examples in the Link Editor and use the Mail link syntax specified to enter the e-mail address in the URL field (**Figure 21**).

3. Close the Link Editor. If you selected text, it is now underlined, indicating that it's a link. If you selected a graphic, a blue border surrounds the image, showing that it's a link (**Figure 22**).

4. Check your work in Preview in Browser mode. Clicking either link should open an e-mail composition window in your browser (**Figure 23**). You'll need to be connected to the Internet to actually compose a message.

✔ Tip

- Remember to use the Link Editor's Link to Recent URL feature if you're linking multiple elements to the same e-mail address.

Setting Anchors

By default, a link carries the user to the top of the destination page. An *anchor* is a placeholder that makes it possible to jump to a specific place on a page. To use anchor links, you must first establish anchors on a page. Then you can link to them.

You can use anchor links to jump from anchor to anchor within a page, or to anchors anywhere in your site.

To create an anchor:

1. In Edit mode, place the insertion point or highlight the text where you want to set an anchor (**Figure 24**).

2. Choose Anchor from the Insert menu, or click the Anchor button on the toolbar. The Anchor Name dialog box appears.

3. Enter a name for the anchor (**Figure 25**).

4. An Anchor icon indicates your anchor's position (**Figure 26**). This icon appears only in Edit mode.

✔ Tips

■ Don't use a number sign to start an anchor name. HTML uses them to link to anchors, and extra number signs can create problems.

■ If you highlighted a text block to make it an anchor, Home Page names the anchor using this text. Otherwise Home Page calls the link *anchor*. You'll want a more distinct name, so overwrite this default name with a new name or number, then click OK to close the dialog box.

Anchor

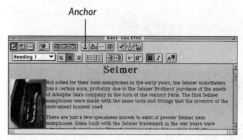

Figure 24. Placing an anchor defines a position within the page to which a link can jump.

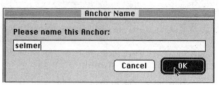

Figure 25. By default Home Page names these links simply *anchor*. You can rename them more appropriately, then click OK.

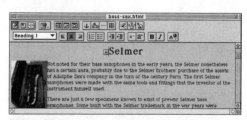

Figure 26. The anchor icon indicates the position defined by the anchor. The icon displays only in Edit mode, not in Preview or Preview in Browser modes.

SETTING ANCHORS

Figure 27. You can use anchors placed at each section of a lengthy page to make a hypertext table of contents.

Figure 28. Select the first item in the table of contents list to create your first anchor link.

Figure 29. When you choose the document you're working on from the Link to Open File submenu, a list of the anchors you've set up appears.

Linking to Anchors within a Page

One popular use of anchors is to create a table of contents at the top of a page with links to different sections of that page. This is especially useful when your page is long and includes several sections.

To create a table of contents, you must first set the anchored items and corresponding contents list, link to your anchors, then add links that take the user back to the top of the page at the end of each section.

To create a table of contents with anchors:

1. Set anchors at the beginning of each content section in an open page (**Figure 27**).

2. Type the name of each anchored section at the top of the page and select the first item on the list (**Figure 28**).

3. Click the Link Editor button on the basic toolbar.

   or

   Choose Link to URL from the Insert menu to open the Link Editor.

4. Click and hold the button to the right of the URL window. Select Link to Open File, select the document you're working on, and then select the anchor you want to link to from the submenu (**Figure 29**), and release the mouse button.

5. Close the Link Editor. The linked text is now blue and underlined.

6. Repeat steps 2–5 until you have connected all the items in the contents list with their respective anchors.

Next, you will create the links that refer from the bottom of the anchored sections back to the top of the page.

To create "back to the top" links:

1. At the end of each anchored section, type in text that will link back to the top of the page (**Figure 30**).

2. Select the first "back to the top" text block (**Figure 31**), then click the Link Editor button or choose Link to URL from the Insert menu. The Link Editor opens.

3. Click and hold the button to the right of the URL window, select Link to Open File, then the name of the file you're working on, then Top of Page (**Figure 32**), and release the mouse button.

4. Repeat steps 2 and 3 until you've set all your "back to the top" anchor links.

5. Test your links in Preview mode. Clicking any of the items in your contents list should send you to the referenced section, and clicking the text you typed for returning to the top of the page should take you back to the top.

✔ Tips

■ To remove an anchor from a page, in Edit mode, select the anchor and press Backspace (Windows), or Delete (Mac) (**Figure 33**).

■ You can also use graphics instead of (or alongside) text to make anchor links. The technique is the same: Select the image, open the Link Editor and link to anchors.

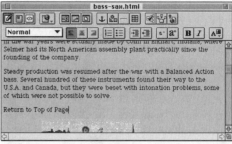

Figure 30. Giving the user a way to return to the table of contents an essential part of this navigational system.

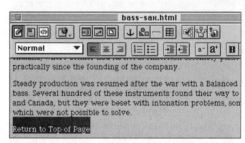

Figure 31. Select the text you typed to make it into an anchor link.

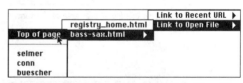

Figure 32. Cascade down from the Link to Open File list to select Top of Page of the file you're working on.

Figure 33. Delete a selected anchor by pressing Backspace (Windows) or Delete (Mac) in Edit mode.

Figure 34. With anchors in place on the destination page, select the text or graphic image you want to use as a link on the source page.

Figure 35. Slide the mouse pointer over to the Open File list's anchors, and select an anchor to link to. Repeat this procedure until all links are made, then test in Preview mode.

Linking to Anchors on Multiple Pages

Linking to anchors on the various pages of your site offers a great way to manage what visitors will see.

To link to an anchor on another page:

1. Open both a source page, which will contain the link, and the destination page. Place anchors on the destination page.

2. In the source page, select either an image or text to link to the anchor on the destination page (**Figure 34**).

3. Click the Link Editor button on the basic toolbar.

   or

   Choose Link to URL from the Insert menu. The Link Editor opens.

4. Click and hold the button to the right of the URL window, select Link to Open File, select the name of the destination document, and select the anchor you want to link to from the submenu (**Figure 35**).

5. Close the Link Editor. Link text will be underlined and blue. Anchored graphics have a blue border around them, indicating a link.

6. Save your pages and test them in Preview or Preview in Browser mode.

Creating an Image Map

Image maps are graphic images with *hot spots*—invisible links to pages on your site or to other locations on the Web. Home Page makes it easy to set up image maps that run on your home machine.

To create a client-side image map:

1. Open a Home Page document that includes the image you would like to map. Double-click the image to open the Image Object Editor. Select the Behavior tab.

2. Select the Image Map radio button, then click Edit to open the Image Map Editor (**Figure 36**).

3. Depending on what shape you want your hot spots to be, select the Rectangular Link tool or the Circular Link tool from Image Map Editor toolbar (**Figure 37**).

4. Click and drag the mouse to define a hot spot location on the image (**Figure 38**), then release the mouse button.

   A black box or circle outlines the area you have defined as a hot spot (**Figure 39**), and the Link Editor opens (**Figure 40**).

5. Enter the URL of your destination page in the URL text window, or click the Browse Files button and select the local file in the resulting dialog box.

   The hot spot's destination URL appears in the Link Editor, and appears over the hot spot link in the Image Map editing window.

6. Repeat steps 4–6 until you've defined all the hot spots in your image (**Figure 41**). The hot spots are numbered on the bottom of each shape you draw.

7. Close the Link Editor.

8. Close the Image Map Editor.

Figure 36. The Image Map Editor opens with your selected GIF image in the preview window, a toolbar on top, and URL settings for setting links.

Figure 37. You can use either the Rectangular Link Tool or the Circular Link Tool to define your hot spots.

Figure 38. Click and drag to define a rectangular hot spot. When you have *surrounded* the area, release the mouse button.

Figure 39. After you release the mouse button, the area you've defined will have a black box around it, complete with resizing handles.

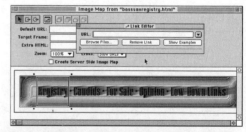

Figure 40. The Image Map Link Editor works exactly like other Link Editors in this chapter, but applies just to defined sections of the image.

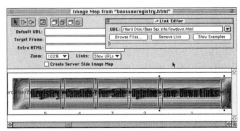

Figure 41. Especially if they're long, the names of the hot links you've defined might display in a rather jumbled fashion.

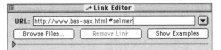

Figure 42. To specify an anchor you want to jump to on a page, add a number sign plus the anchor name to your URL.

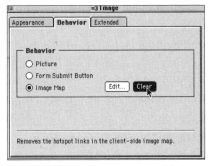

Figure 43. To unmap an image, just click clear.

9. Test your image map in Preview mode, clicking each section of the image and making sure the referenced pages open properly.

✔ Tips

- You can include anchors in the URLs of your hot spot by adding the number sign (#) and the anchor name at the end of the URL (**Figure 42**).

- To remove a hot spot and its referenced URLs from an image map, select the image-mapped graphic. Open the Object Editor by double-clicking, and select the Behavior tab. Then click the Clear button (**Figure 43**).

USING IMAGE MAPS

TABLES

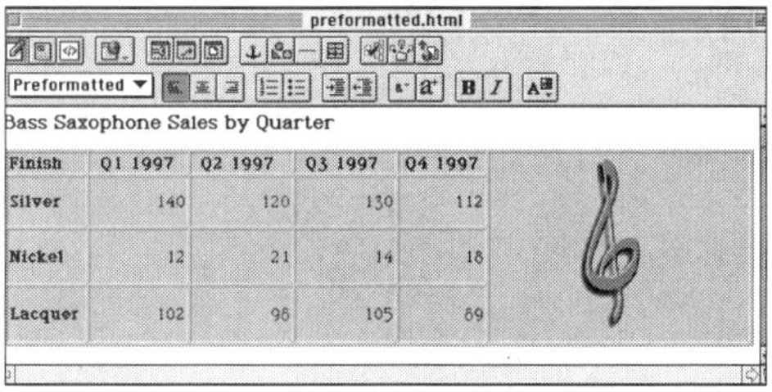

Figure 1. Use tables to organize your material and give it impact. Table cells can hold images as well as text and numbers, and can have their own background colors or background images.

Tables are a good example of the law of unexpected consequences. Table tags were introduced to HTML as a better and easier way to align text, but it didn't take Web designers long to push beyond the intent of HTML's new feature. They began filling tables with images, formatted text (**Figure 1**), and even other tables, using the alignment control tables offer to create multicolumned layout grids (**Figure 2**).

With their increasing complexity, however, tables have become difficult to create using HTML tags. To avoid the hassle, Home Page allows you to simply place a preset default table on your page and customize it for your purposes. In this chapter, you'll learn about tables and how to work with them.

Figure 2. Tables allow designers to mimic multicolumn, magazine-style layouts.

Creating Tables

In HTML, tables are made up of rows and cells—that's it. Home Page translates this into the familiar concept of rows and columns for you. With Home Page, you can add tables to your page in two different ways: by creating an empty table to which you add text and images (**Figure 3**), or by pasting in table data you've copied from a spreadsheet or database program and letting Home Page automatically create a table to contain it (**Figure 4**).

To insert an empty table:

In Edit mode, position the insertion point where you want to place the table, then choose Table from the Insert menu.

or

Click the Insert Table button on the Basic toolbar.

A table appears at the insertion point, and the Table Object Editor opens (**Figure 5**).

✔ Tip

- You can also click and drag the Table button onto your page where you want to place your table and release the mouse button. With this method, the Table Object Editor does not automatically open.

Insert Table button

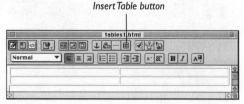

Figure 3. Click the Insert Table button on the Basic toolbar to place a table. The default table layout is two columns wide and two rows deep.

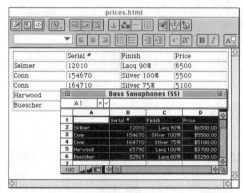

Figure 4. This spreadsheet data has been copied from Claris Works and pasted into Home Page, which automatically creates a table to fit it.

Figure 5. The Table Object Editor opens when you use the Insert menu or a single-click of the table button to place a table.

CREATING TABLES

Figure 6. The Table Object Editor is where you change a selected table's attributes, such as the number of columns and rows.

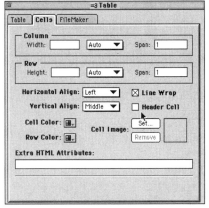

Figure 7. The Cells tab allows you to change the attributes of individual selected cells.

Object Editor button

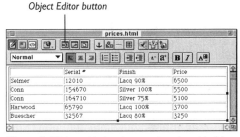

Figure 8. Click a table border to select the table. Note the rule around the table, with three handles (the small black boxes) for dragging and resizing the table.

Opening the Table Object Editor

In Home Page, the default table configuration is unformatted, left-aligned text in two rows and two columns. If that's what you need, you're set. If you need something different, your next step is to use the Table Object Editor to customize your table.

You can change the attributes of an entire table using the settings in the Object Editor's Table tab (**Figure 6**), or change the attributes of individual cells using the Cells tab (**Figure 7**).

When you select a single cell and open the Object Editor, you see three tabs: Table, Cells, and FileMaker. When the entire table is selected, the only two tabs shown are Table and FileMaker. You will learn more about the FileMaker tab in Chapter 11.

To open the Table Object Editor:

1. Double-click either the outside border of a table or a single table cell.

   or

   Select either the entire table or a single table cell, and click the Object Editor button on the toolbar (**Figure 8**).

2. Select the different tabs to view the available options (more on these tabs in the following pages).

✔ Tip

■ Be careful working with tables. You can accidentally delete a table or cell after you have selected it by pressing [Bksp] (Windows) or [Delete] (Mac). If this happens, immediately press [Ctrl] [Z] (Windows) or [⌘] [Z] (Mac) to undo the deletion.

Changing Table Attributes

The Object Editor's Table tab controls the most common attributes of your tables. **Table 1** describes the different elements of the Table tab and what they do. The steps on the next few pages tell you how to use them.

To change the number of rows or columns in a table:

1. Double-click the table, or select it and click the Object Editor button, to open the Table Object Editor.

2. In the Rows field, enter the number of rows you want in your table (**Figure 9**).
   or
   Click the Add Row and Remove Row buttons in the Table Object Editor until you have the desired number of rows.

3. In the Columns field, enter the number of vertical columns you want in your table.
   or
   Click the Add Column and Remove Column buttons until you have the desired number of columns.

4. Close the Table Object Editor.

✔ Tip

- Tables in Home page can be up to 100 rows by 100 columns in size.

Table 1.
The Table Object Editor: The Table tab

ELEMENT	WHAT IT DOES
Rows	Changes the number of rows in a table. Enter the number of rows in a window, or use the buttons to add and remove rows one at a time.
Columns	Changes the number of columns in a table. Enter the number of columns in a window, or use the buttons to add and remove columns one at a time.
Width	Changes a table's width, either in pixels (an absolute measurement) or as a percentage of the browser window. Also includes a relative setting for making the table fit evenly around all table elements.
Height	Changes a table's height, either in pixels or as a percentage of the browser.
Spacing	Controls the amount of space between cells by controlling the width of the cell border.
Padding	Controls the amount of space between the contents of the cells and the cell border.
Border	Determines the width and appearance of the border elements in a table.
Table Color	Assigns a color to use as the table's background.
Table Image	Assigns an image to use as the table's background.
Extra HTML Attributes.	Adds more capabilities for users well-versed in HTML.

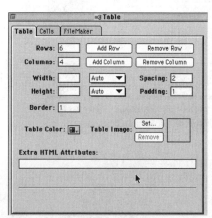

Figure 9. Enter the desired number of rows and columns in the respective fields in the Table Object Editor.

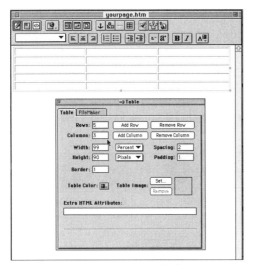

Figure 10. As with rows and columns, you can change the width and height of a table by entering width and height in pixels, as a percentage of a browser window, or by selecting Auto, which gives the table a width and height that fits evenly around its elements.

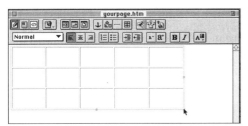

Figure 11. Click and drag one of the table's resizing handles to change its dimensions.

To change a table's width or height:

1. Double-click the table, or select it and click the Object Editor button, to open the Table Object Editor.

2. In the Width and Height windows, enter the desired table dimensions, either in pixels or as a percentage of the browser window. Or enter Auto, which gives the table a width and height that fits evenly around its elements (**Figure 10**).

3. Close the Table Object Editor.

To size tables manually by dragging sizing handles:

1. Click once on the table to select it.

2. Drag the bottom handle to change the height of the table.
   Drag the handle on the right side of the table to change the width.

3. Drag the lower right-hand handle (**Figure 11**) to change the height and width of the table at the same time.

✔ Tip

■ If you set an absolute width and height for your table, make sure you make it a size that will work on smaller (15 inch) screens so your viewers can see all the data without scrolling.

Adding Text to a Table

You can add text directly to a table cell, or copy and paste it from another document (**Figure 12**).

To type text directly into a cell:

1. In your Home Page document, click on the cell where you want to insert text. The cell's outline becomes bold, and a flashing insertion point appears.

2. Type in your text and format it using the techniques described in Chapter 3 (**Figure 13**).

To paste text into a cell from another document:

1. Click on the cell where you want to insert text. The cell's outline becomes bold, and a flashing insertion point appears.

2. After copying or cutting text from another document, choose Paste from the File menu.

✔ Tips

■ Text formatted in and copied from another Home Page document will keep its formatting. When you paste in text from another application, its formatting won't always carry over.

■ When adding a large column of text to a cell, consider changing the value of the Border to 0 in the Table Object Editor. This creates a clean, publication-like grid. The grid will appear as dotted lines when in Edit mode (**Figure 14**).

Figure 12. Notice that the table cell automatically resizes itself to fit when you format the text.

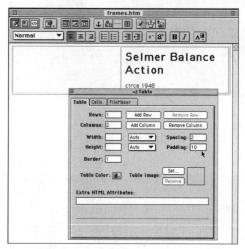

Figure 13. To prevent left-aligned text from colliding with cell walls, enter a higher number in the padding window of the Table Object Editor.

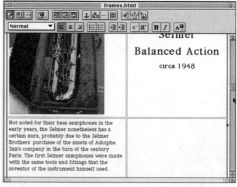

Figure 14. Borderless frames create the effect of a publication grid. The dotted lines will disappear when you view your page in Preview mode or in a browser.

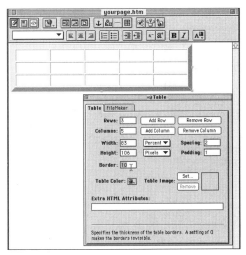

Figure 15. The table border is shaded to make it appear beveled. The greater the value in the Border field, the more the table appears to rise from the page.

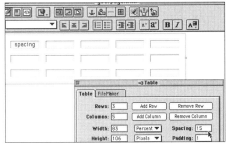

Figure 16. Spacing affects the area between individual table cells.

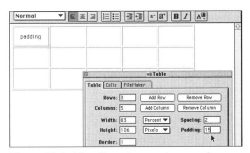

Figure 17. Padding affects the space between the contents of a cell and the cell border.

Table Border, Spacing, and Padding

Table spacing and borders are controlled by three fields in the Table Object Editor: *Border*, *Spacing*, and *Padding*. The Border setting determines the outline of the table (**Figure 15**). Spacing controls the space between table cells (**Figure 16**). Padding determines the area between a cell wall and its contents (**Figure 17**). For each of these attributes, you can enter any value between 0 and 100.

To change a table's border settings:

1. Double-click the table, or select it and click the Object Editor button, to open the Table Object Editor.

2. Select the Table tab and enter a new value for Border, Spacing, or Padding.

3. Close the Table Object Editor.

✔ Tips

- Enter a border value of 0 to make your table border invisible, creating an invisible layout grid.

- If you select a border of 0, you will see a dotted line defining the cells when in Edit mode. When you switch to Preview mode or Preview in Browser mode, the borders are not visible.

TABLE BORDER, SPACING, AND PADDING

Creating Tables with Copied Data

Home Page allows you to copy and paste tables directly from your spreadsheet program, and to import data directly from a database file. In each instance, Home Page automatically creates a table to fit the pasted content.

Figure 18. In your spreadsheet application, select and copy the data you will be displaying in your Home Page table on the Web.

To create a table with data from a spreadsheet application:

1. Open both your Home Page document and the spreadsheet document that has the table data you want to place on your page.

2. In your spreadsheet document, select and copy the table data you want to place in a table (**Figure 18**).

3. In your Home Page document, position the insertion point on your page where you want the table to appear.

4. Choose Paste from the Edit menu. A table containing your data appears (**Figure 19**), and the Table Object Editor opens.

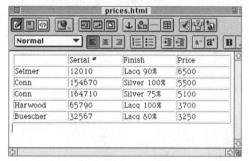

Figure 19. Choose Paste from the Edit menu to add the copied spreadsheet information to your Web page.

To create a table with data from a database application:

1. Open both your Home Page document and the database document that has the table data you want to place on your page.

2. Save the database table data as tab-delimited text and open the resulting file in a word processor.

3. Select and copy the tab-delimited table data.

4. In your Home Page document, position the insertion point on your page where you want the table to appear.

5. Choose Paste from the Edit menu. A table containing your data appears on your page, and the Table Object Editor opens.

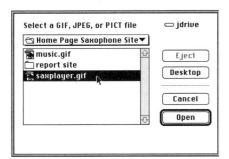

Figure 20. You can select any GIF, JPEG, or PICT image to put in your table cell.

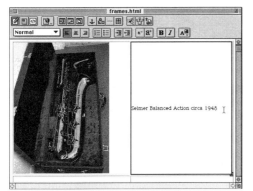

Figure 21. Since tables resize according to their contents, you may find it easiest to place all your images before formatting the text or manually resizing the tables.

Inserting Images into a Table

Images can appear in a cell in one of two ways: either as cell contents or acting as a background.

To add an image to a cell:

1. Select the cell, choose Image from the Insert menu, then select an image file from the dialog box, and click OK (**Figure 20**).

   or

   Copy and paste in an image from another document.

   The image appears in the selected cell (**Figure 21**).

2. Resize the image as needed, either manually using your mouse, or by double-clicking the image and adjusting it in the Image Object Editor.

✔ Tip

■ A table image can act as an anchor, using the techniques described in Chapter 5.

Changing a Table Background

The Table Object Editor gives you control of the background of your table. You can add color and images, making your page more lively and attractive.

To change the background color of a table:

1. Double-click a table to open the Table Object Editor, and select the Table tab.

2. Click and hold the Table Color button to open the drop-down color palette (**Figure 22**).

3. Choose a new color by selecting it with the mouse pointer and releasing the mouse button.

To return the background color to the default color:

1. Double-click a table to open the Table Object Editor.

2. Click and hold the Table Color button to open the drop-down color palette, and select Default (**Figure 23**).

✔ Tip

■ The entire table can have a background, or individual cells and rows can have their own colors. There is more on setting color in cells and rows later in this chapter.

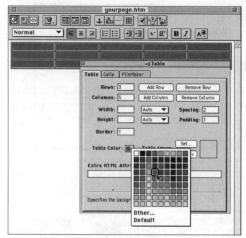

Figure 22. Home Page offers you a full spectrum of background colors.

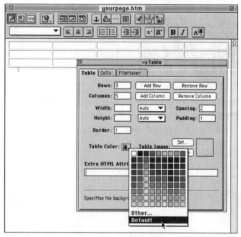

Figure 23. If you are unhappy with the color you've chosen, start over by selecting Default.

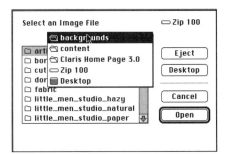

Figure 24. Home Page comes with a wide variety of background images. You can find them in the backgrounds folder in the content directory in your Home Page folder.

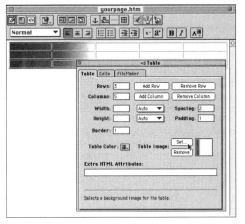

Figure 25. Notice that a thumbnail of your chosen background appears next to the set button. This is useful when you are working with gradients or watermarks.

To use a background image in a table:

1. Double-click a table to open the Table Object Editor, and select the Table tab.

2. Click Set in the Table Image section.
The Select an Image File dialog box opens.

3. Select a background-image file (**Figure 24**) and click Open.

The background image appears in the table (**Figure 25**).

To remove a background image:

1. Double-click a table to open the Table Object Editor, and select the Table tab.

2. Click Remove in the Table Image section.

✔ Tip

■ When you publish your site, the background image file should be in your images directory. You can do this manually, or use the Consolidate feature, which is covered in Chapter 9.

Changing Cell Attributes

Cells have their own set of attributes and their own tab in the Table Object Editor to control them. **Table 2** describes the different elements of the Cells tab and what they do. The following pages tell you how to use them.

To view the Cells tab of the Table Object Editor:

1. Open a Home Page file that contains a table.

2. Double-click a cell to select it and open the Table Object Editor. The Cells tab is selected (**Figure 26**).

✔ Tips

- You can leave the Table Object Editor open and switch back and forth between the Table and Cell tabs.

- As your page layouts get more complex, be sure to check your pages on the two common browsers to make sure they're displaying correctly.

- Virtually everything you can do to a single cell can be performed to a group of adjacent cells at the same time.

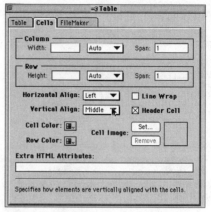

Figure 26. The Cells tab of the Table Object Editor has a few features that differ from the Table tab, such as Span and Vertical and Horizontal Alignment. Notice that you can find a definition of an element by passing your mouse over it.

Table 2.
The Table Object Editor: The Cells tab

ELEMENT	WHAT IT DOES
Column	Contains settings for width, expressed in pixels, as a percentage of the browser window, or Auto for even distribution, plus a Span setting that combines vertically connected cells into a single cell.
Row	Contains settings for height, expressed in pixels, percent, or Auto, plus a Span setting that combines horizontally connected cells into a single cell.
Horizontal Align	Aligns the contents of a cell either to the left, center, or right.
Vertical Align	Aligns the contents of a cell either to the top, middle, baseline, or bottom.
Line Wrap	Wraps text within a cell.
Header Cell	Makes the selected cell a column head, which appears in boldface.
Cell Color	Assigns color to an individual cell.
Row Color	Assigns color to the entire row where the selected cell is located.
Cell Image: Set	Sets a background image within a cell.
Cell Image: Remove	Removes a background image from a cell.
Graphic Image Preview Box	Displays background image in the selected cell.
Extra HTML Attributes Text Field	Used to add additional HTML features.

Figure 27. To resize a cell, you can select any of its four boundaries and then change its width or height by dragging it.

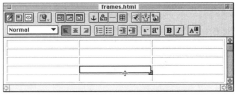

Figure 28. The cursor displays arrows that show how the cell will resize.

To resize a cell:

1. Select the cell you want to resize.

2. Click and drag one of the vertical edges to make the cell wider (**Figure 27**), or click and drag one of the horizontal edges to make the cell deeper (**Figure 28**).

   or

1. Double-click the cell to open the Table Object Editor.

2. Enter the new size values in the Width and Height fields. Insert a number of pixels to make the cell a fixed size, or a percentage to size the cell relative to the browser window; or choose Auto, the default setting, which divides the table into cells of equal size.

To resize multiple cells:

1. Select the first cell.

2. Shift-click the last cell. A group of cells must be adjacent to each other.

3. Click and drag the selected cells using the sizing handles.

✔ Tips

■ Changing a cell's width will change the width of the entire column in which the cell is located. Similarly, changing the height of a cell will change the height of that cell's entire row.

■ When you add text and images to your table, the table cells will resize themselves automatically to match the size of the text or image.

RESIZING TABLE CELLS

To use an image as a cell background:

1. Double-click the cell in which you want to place a background to open the Table Object Editor, and choose the Cells tab.

2. Click the Set button (**Figure 29**). The Select an Image File dialog box opens.

3. Select the image file to use as the cell background (**Figure 30**).

4. Close the Table Object Editor.

   The selected cell now displays the image you chose as a background (**Figure 31**).

✔ Tips

- An image background is just that, a background. You can add things on top of it, such as text, or even other images (**Figure 32**).

- Unlike other images in table cells, you cannot use a background image as an anchor or a link.

Figure 29. The Set button sits in the Cell Image area of the Table Object Editor's Cell tab.

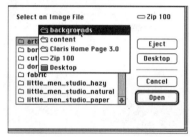

Figure 30. Home Page provides a number of backgrounds. You can find them in the backgrounds folder of the content directory.

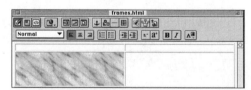

Figure 31. The best backgrounds are subtle images with a continuous tone.

Figure 32. Once you've added a background, you can add other elements on top of it.

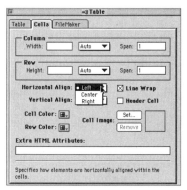

Figure 33. Using the Table Object Editor's Cell tab, you can align text horizontally to the left, right, or center.

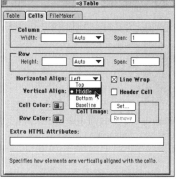

Figure 34. The Vertical alignment options are described in **Table 4.**

Changing Cell Alignment

You can align images and text horizontally in a cell the same way you do outside of one. Select the text or image and click an alignment button, or choose an alignment from the Format menu. You can also use the Horizontal Align drop-down menu in the Cells tab to set alignment (**Figure 33**).

You can also vertically align cell elements (**Figure 34**) to the top, middle, or bottom of the cell, and control baseline alignment, which prevents clipping off the descenders of some characters (g, j, y) when the cell contains just one line of text (**Tables 3** and **4**).

To align text and images in a cell:

1. Select the cell that contains the element you want to align. This element can be text or an image.

2. Double-click the cell, or select it and click the Object Editor button, to open the Table Object Editor, and select the Cells tab.

3. Choose an alignment setting from either the Horizontal Align or Vertical Align drop-down lists.

4. Close the Table Object Editor.

Table 3. Horizontal alignment options in the Table Object Editor's Cells tab

ALIGNMENT	WHAT IT DOES
Left	Aligns the cell elements to the left.
Right	Aligns the elements to the right.
Center	Aligns the elements to the center.

Table 4. Vertical alignment options in the Table Object Editor's Cells tab

ALIGNMENT	WHAT IT DOES
Top	Aligns the cell elements to the top.
Middle	Aligns the elements to the middle.
Bottom	Aligns the elements to the bottom.
Baseline	Prevents descenders of single lines of text from colliding with cell walls.

CHANGING CELL ALIGNMENT

Spanning Multiple Cells

You can format a single cell so that it spans more than one cell's width or height. Spanning is a common way to make a heading for a multicolumn table. It is also an appealing design technique when using a zero-pixel border-table to emulate a publication grid (**Figure 35**).

To change the span of a cell:

1. Select the cell you want to span by clicking it. A heavy black border indicates that the cell is selected (**Figure 36**).

2. Double-click the cell, or select it and click the Object Editor button, to open the Table Object Editor. The Cells tab will already be selected.

3. In the Span window of either the Column or Row sections, enter the number of cells you want the selected cell to span.

4. Close the Table Object Editor. The cell now spans the specified number of cells (**Figure 37**).

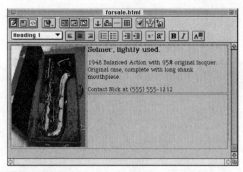

Figure 35. The cell with the image on the left spans two rows.

Selected cell border

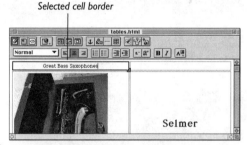

Figure 36. You can tell when a cell is selected by the thick black border surrounding it.

Figure 37. The top cell here spans two columns to create a headline effect.

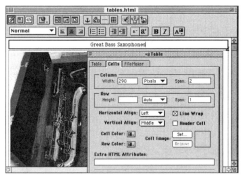

Figure 38. Header cells are used to top table columns. One common place to use them is atop a set of spanned cells.

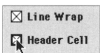

Figure 39. The Header cell button is below Line Wrap in the Table Object Editor's Cells tab.

Using Header Cells

Header Cells are often used in conjunction with spanned cells to provide a header for the table (**Figure 38**). Header cells display in bold text in most Web browsers.

To set a header cell:

1. Type the text into a spanned cell you want to use as a header.

2. Click an alignment button on the toolbar.

   or

   Choose an alignment from the alignment submenu in the Format menu to align your text.

3. Double-click the cell to Open the Table Object Editor.

4. Select the Header Cell check box (**Figure 39**). The text in the header cell will be displayed as bold text.

BEYOND BASIC TRAINING

Figure 1. Home Page's installed libraries are full of prefab goodies.

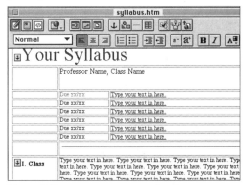

Figure 2. Site templates give you a head start on many common Web page formats.

If you've read the early chapters, you know most of what it takes to set up a Web page using Home Page's arsenal of easy-to-use tools. Now you'll learn about more advanced features that make page and site building even easier.

In this chapter you'll learn about time-saving features such as *libraries*, where you can store page elements for drag-and-drop insertion onto multiple pages; reusable *templates* that reduce your design time to almost nothing; and *site assistants* that walk you through the site-building process step by step.

Using Libraries and Elements

Libraries are collections of elements. Libraries allow you to view elements in an organized, filing cabinet-like window, then simply drag the one you choose to your page to place it.

Elements are anything you can place on a Web page: text, images, QuickTime movies, animated GIFs—you get the idea. And if it's an element, then you can store it in a library.

Along with using Home Page's libraries, it makes good sense to create your own library to give you quick access to the recurring elements you use in a project.

To place an element using a library:

1. Open a Home Page document.

2. Choose Library from the File menu, then choose one of the libraries listed in the resulting submenu (**Figure 3**). All libraries include an .hlb filename extension.

3. Select a library entry from the left column of the library window by clicking it (**Figure 4**).

4. When you've selected the entry, scroll through its contents (shown on the right side of the library window) using the right column's vertical scroll bar.

5. Select an element to place on your page, and click, drag, and drop it onto the open page.

   or

   Select the image, then click and hold the Insert in Page button, revealing a drop-down list showing all open files (**Figure 5**). Choose the page you want to place the element in and release the mouse button.

Figure 3. When stored in the contents folder in your Home Page application folder, libraries are available through the Library submenu.

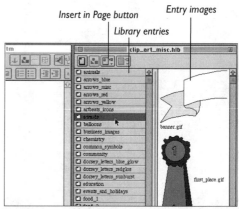

Figure 4. The list of available library entries appears on the left side of the library window; the images included in the entries appear on the right.

Figure 5. Insert an element onto a page using the Insert in Page button.

Use as Page Background button

Figure 6. Make sure you select the image for your background before using the Use as Page Background drop-down list.

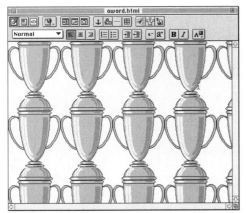

Figure 7. If the image you select for a background is large enough, it fills the whole screen. Otherwise, the image tiles to fill the page.

Tool Status Line

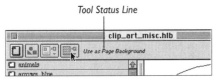

Figure 8. Look for the Tool Status line in many of Home Page's windows for hints about what buttons do.

To use a library image as a background:

1. Choose Library from the File menu, then choose one of the libraries from the Library submenu.

2. Select a library entry from the list on the left of the library window, and an image from the images on the right.

3. Click and hold the Use as Page Background button at the top of the library window. A drop-down list appears showing all open Home Page files (**Figure 6**).

4. Select the file you want to place the background in and release the mouse button.

The image is now the background image for the page (**Figure 7**).

✔ Tips

■ Just like the Home Page main window, the library window has a Tool Status line that tells you what its buttons do when you place the cursor over them (**Figure 8**).

■ For a collection of entries made specifically to be used as backgrounds, select the backgrounds.hlb file from the Library menu.

■ The library window stays open and available until you close it.

USING A LIBRARY IMAGE AS A BACKGROUND

To create a new library file and add entries:

1. Choose Library from the File menu, then choose New from the resulting submenu.

   A new library window appears, called untitled.hlb. The left side of the library window contains a library entry, called *untitled* (**Figure 9**).

2. Double-click the untitled entry to high-light it, then enter a new name (**Figure 10**) for it.

3. To add more entries, click the New Entry button on the Library window toolbar and name them using step 2 until you have all the entries you want. You can add a new entry at any time.

✔ Tip

■ You can store all the elements you want to put in this library in one big entry, or create multiple entries for organizing similar elements such as text, graphics, and QuickTime movies.

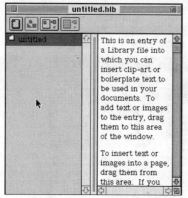

Figure 9. Both the new library and the new library entry are called *untitled.*

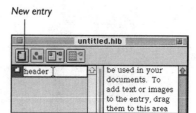

Figure 10. This library entry is called header, where various header elements will be stored.

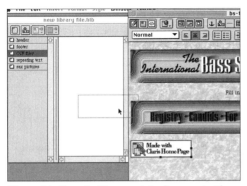

Figure 11. Place the library and the document with elements side by side for easier dragging and dropping.

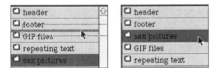

Figure 12. Just move a library entry with your mouse to put it in a new place in the lineup.

To add elements to a library:

1. Place both the library and the document that includes the element(s) you want to add to the library on the desktop, and select the element you want to add (**Figure 11**).

2. Drag the element across the desktop to the right column of the library window and release the mouse button.

   The element appears in the library window, and is now part of the highlighted entry in the library file.

3. When you've finished, save and name your library, including the .hlb extension. Remember to save it in the contents folder of your Claris Home Page folder so it will be available through the Library submenu.

✔ Tips

- Remember, elements can be text, graphics, tables, pieces of HTML code—whatever you want to keep handy while you build your pages.

- You can drag and drop elements into a library from almost any application. If drag and drop doesn't work, try copying and pasting.

- To change the order in which entries appear in a library, select an entry and drag it into a new position (**Figure 12**).

- To place all the elements in a library entry onto a page at once, select the entry name, making sure no elements in the right-hand column are selected. Then drag and drop the entry name onto an open page.

- To change an entry name, double-click it and type in a new name.

- To delete an entry, select the entry by clicking it once and press (Backspace) (Windows), or (Delete) (Mac), or choose Clear from the Edit menu.

Using Templates

Templates are Home Page files that include preformatted attributes and elements that can save you a lot of design time. You can use one of Home Page's templates, or choose a page or site you design and save it to reuse as a template.

Home Page installs a collection of templates. There are 13 useful pages and 7 full-blown sites, the most advanced of which features animations and Java roll-over buttons. They're found in the site_template and page_template folders in your Claris Home Page application folder. Or, if you have a page you've slaved over, you can keep its format for reuse as a template.

To open a template:

1. Choose New from the File menu. The New dialog box opens.

2. Select Use Template, then scroll through the list of templates to find the one you want to use (**Figure 13**). A brief description of the template appears under the template list.

3. Click OK. The template opens and is called untitled.html (**Figure 14**).

4. Edit the file to make the content your own. Treat this page like any other—edit it, name it, save it, and make it part of a site.

Figure 13. Home Page has both single page and full site templates to choose from.

Figure 14. Once it's open, you can change any template element to suit your needs using basic page-creation techniques.

Figure 15. Save a page as a template to reuse it later.

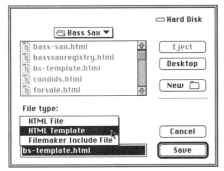

Figure 16. Opening a file you've saved as a template creates an untitled page with set features.

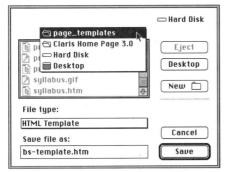

Figure 17. You must save your template in the page_templates folder for it to function properly.

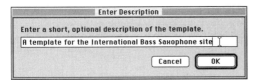

Figure 18. Enter a description of your template.

To save a page as a template:

1. Open the page you want to save and reuse as a template.

2. To simplify your template, remove specific text from the page and replace it with generic text such as "Place text here" (**Figure 15**).

3. Choose Save As from the File menu, then select HTML Template from the File type drop-down list (**Figure 16**), and enter the template name into the Save File As field.

4. If you want your template to be available along with Home Page's other templates, save your file in the page_templates folder inside the Claris Home Page application folder (**Figure 17**).

5. Click Save.

   A dialog box prompts you for a brief description of the template (**Figure 18**). This is the (optional) description that appears when you highlight your template in the list of template options.

6. Click OK to close this dialog box, and your template is ready for use.

✔ Tip

■ In order for a new template to appear in the collection of included templates, you must quit and relaunch Home Page.

Using Site Assistants

Home Page's site assistants walk you through every step of the site building process, turning less-than-pleasant tasks into handy question-and-answer sessions that automatically set up your site structure for you.

There are six different site types you can build with the help of a site assistant (**Table 1**). This section shows how to work with most of them. You will learn to use the Frame assistant in Chapter 8, and the FileMaker Connection assistant in Chapter 11.

To create a site using a site assistant:

1. Close all open files in Home Page and choose New (not New Page) from the File menu.

2. Click the Use Assistant button and select the site you want to build from the list that appears below it. Note that a description of each site displays below the list as you scroll through it (**Figure 19**).

3. Click OK.

   The site assistant's first screen appears, informing you what the assistant can do.

4. Click Next.

   The assistant starts its Q & A mode. With the School site assistant (**Figure 20**), you're asked the name of the school and given several check boxes that let you decide which pages to include in your site.

   The site map on the left shows the hierarchy of the pages you'll be creating.

5. When you have selected all the pages you want for your site, click Next.

6. Continue through each assistant page, filling in the text fields and selecting the check boxes according to your needs.

Table 1. The site assistants

ASSISTANT	WHAT IT DOES
Frame	Creates a frames page.
FileMaker	Creates a dynamic Web page, powered by FileMaker 4.0.
Newsletter	Creates a Web-based newsletter, complete with a hypertext TOC.
Personal Site	Helps you set up a Web site that displays things like family photos and stories, and favorite links pages.
Presentation	Creates a business presentation for displaying products and services.
Report	Creates a report site with a Table of Contents, Bibliography, and other useful pages.
School Site	Makes a site for an entire school including classroom, departments, and links pages.
Standard Site	Creates a simple generic site with anchors and links.

Figure 19. Choose a site assistant from the list.

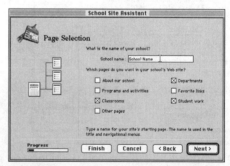

Figure 20 The site assistants lead you through building a site in a Q & A format. Note the Progress indicator in the lower-left corner of the window. It tells you how far along you are in the process.

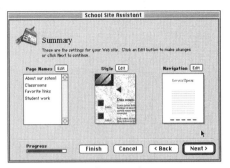

Figure 21. One last chance to change your settings.

Figure 22. Click one of the folder location choices.

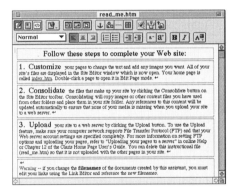

Figure 23. The read_me file tells you what you need to do to finish your site.

Figure 24. Enter your text over the placeholders.

7. After the last assistant page, the site assistant's Summary displays what you've chosen and gives you one more opportunity to change your settings by clicking one of the Edit buttons (**Figure 21**). When they're all to your liking, click Next.

8. Next, a Location window asks if you want the files the assistant generates to be placed in a new or an existing folder (**Figure 22**).

If you've already created a site folder, click Existing folder, navigate to your folder, and select it. If you want to create a new folder, click the New Folder button, name your folder, and click Save.

9. Click Create in the Assistant window.

The site assistant now generates several files, including an HTML file called read_me, which automatically launches when you're done creating your site (**Figure 23**). The file summarizes the steps you must take to finish your site. The assistant has done its job, which is to set up and link the structure and pages for your site.

To finish your site:

1. Enter your text and insert images. The text and graphics are blocked out so you can see where they should go (**Figure 24**).

2. Upload your site to the server, which you'll learn to do in Chapter 9.

✔ Tip

■ Once you're comfortable with the contents of your site folder—and once you've performed all the tasks read_me.htm tells you to do—delete read_me.htm.

FRAMES

Navigational frame   *Content frame*   *Header frame*

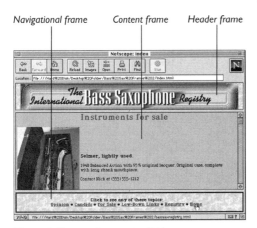

Figure 1. Frames allow you to divide your screen into separate windows that work independently. In this case, frames allow both the headline image and the navigational frame at the bottom to remain in place as the user scrolls through the content frame in the center.

Perhaps the greatest challenge facing Web designers is figuring out how to make their user interface a creative and efficient one. *Frames* are one way to do this. Frames allow you to designate separate windows within a single browser window for content such as headers, site navigation links (often called *navbars*), and various content files (**Figure 1**). Together, the independent areas of a frames-based page are called *framesets*. Each frame in a frameset is just like its own Web page, with its own source file and scroll bars.

Frames are another advanced HTML technique made simple by Home Page.

✔ Tips

- Frames may not display on certain browsers, and might display differently from browser to browser.

- Frames can fill up space in the browser window quickly. More than two frames can be excessive for a 15-inch monitor.

- Frames do sneaky things to browsers' bookmark functionality. Visitors return to a frame layout and not the HTML page they have bookmarked.

- You can simulate many of the functional uses of frames using tables.

Creating a Basic Frame Layout

Home Page's Frames Assistant offers the simplest way to create a frames layout.

The frame-based page you'll learn to create in the following series of steps is a common one, including in its frameset navigational, header, and main content frames. The navigational frame is a dynamic table of contents with links to your site content; the header frame contains text or images that you want to appear on all your pages; and the main content frame displays the various files linked to from your navigational frame TOC. Before you start creating a frames-based site, you should put all the images and HTML files you will use in one site folder.

To set up your frameset layout:

1. Prepare the files you want to use in your frameset and collect them in one folder, with all of the images in their own folder.

2. Choose New from the File menu.

3. Select the Use Assistant button, select Frame Page from the list, and click OK.

4. The Frame Assistant window opens. Read the Overview (**Figure 2**), then click Next.

5. Select the frameset layout you want to use, then click Next.(**Figure 3**).The Navigational Frame Selection window opens.

6. Select the frame you want to use for your navigational frame, then click Next (**Figure 4**).Take note which frame you choose (A, B, or C), you'll need this information later.

7. Confirm your frame selection in the next window, then click Next.

Continuing with the Frame Assistant, next you'll determine the content that will appear in the header and main frames, automatically linked to from the navigational frame.

Figure 2. The Overview screen gives you a rundown of the steps the assistant will take you through.

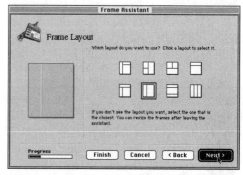

Figure 3. The Frame Assistant offers a number of standard frame layouts.The thumbnail picture on the left side of the window reflects the selected layout.

Figure 4. The assistant lets you choose which frame will contain your hyperlinked table of contents.

Figure 5. The Frames File list truncates file names, so if you need to look at a file name, make sure you do so before you click the Add button.

Figure 6. The Location screen displays the location of your new pages below the New Folder and Existing Folder buttons.

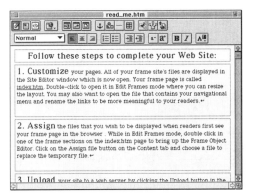

Figure 7. The read_me file tells you what you'll need to do to complete your frame-based page.

To add content to your frameset:

1. Click Browse in the Assign Files window, select a file you want to appear in the selected frame (outlined in blue on the left side of the Frame Assistant window) from the selection window, and click Open. The file and its path appear in the File name field.

   If this is your header frame and you want just one static image or text file to appear here, click Next to proceed to assigning the main frame content. The second frame is highlighted in the Frame Assistant window.

2. Click Browse, select a file you want to appear in this frame, and click Open. The file and its path appear in the File name field. Repeat this procedure until you have assigned all the files you want to display in this frame and they appear in the Frame Files list (**Figure 5**).

   To remove a file from the list, highlight it and click Remove.

3. Click Next.

Next, you'll choose the location for your site.

To choose the location of your site:

1. The Location window asks you to designate the location of the folder containing your frame content. Select the folder where you've gathered your site files.

2. Click Create (**Figure 6**). The Frame Assistant prepares the site and automatically opens a read_me file (**Figure 7**). Note that there is a hypertext link to index.htm, and read through this file. Its contents are covered later in this and following chapters.

To select frame default files:

1. With the read_me file open, click the Preview mode button, then click index.htm.

   or

   Double-click the index.htm file in the Site Editor window.

2. The frame page index.htm, opens (**Figure 8**) in a special Edit Frames mode, as indicated by an added mode button in the toolbar. Make sure this button is selected (**Figure 9**).

3. If you have one, double-click your header frame. The Frame Object Editor opens with the Content tab selected.

4. Click the Assign File button (**Figure 10**), select the file you want to appear in your header frame, and click Open.

5. Double-click the main content frame. The Frame Object Editor opens with the Content tab selected.

6. Click the Assign File button, navigate to and select the file you want to appear in this frame when a visitor first comes to your site, and click Open.

   This file can be one you've already referenced in your navigational frame, or it can be another file. The difference is that the file you assign here will not automatically appear in your navigational frame.

7. Close the Frame Object Editor. The selected primary page appears (**Figure 11**).

Now, you must edit the names in the navigational menu so that your user knows where the links lead.

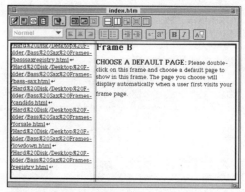

Figure 8. One frame contains a list of linked file locations, the other explains how to replace what's there now with a real page.

Figure 9. The Edit Frames mode button appears only when you're working on frame pages.

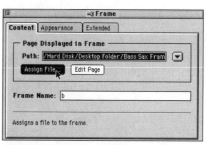

Figure 10. The path to the file you select using the Browse button appears in the Path field.

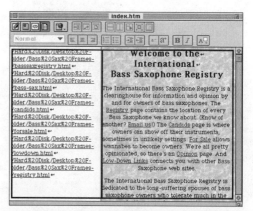

Figure 11. The selected primary file, generally your site's home page, appears where Frame B once was.

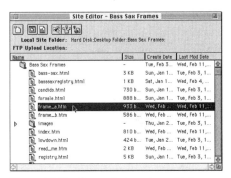

Figure 12. The Frames Assistant has added new files to your site including frame files, and index file, and a read_me file.

Figure 13. You can edit the names of your navigational links directly in Edit mode.

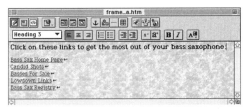

Figure 14. Add any design features or introductory text to match the style and tone of the files that will appear in the content frame.

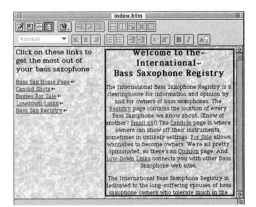

Figure 15. The navigational items should be descriptive so visitors know where they're going.

To edit the navigational menu:

1. Double-click your navigational frame file (frame_a.htm, frame_b.htm, or frame_c.htm) in the Site Editor window (**Figure 12**).

or

Choose Open from the file menu and select your navigational frame.

2. The file opens in Edit mode containing the navigational links you've assigned (**Figure 13**). Highlight the linked text blocks one by one and replace them with descriptive terms.

When you select the linked text, make sure you highlight only the link, not the paragraph return symbol, or else the new text you type might not contain the linked information. You can tell that the new text is a link if it's underlined and blue. If it isn't, undo your action and try again.

3. Add a title to your Navigational Frame by entering and formatting text and if you wish, use the Document Options button to add a background color or image (**Figure 14**).

4. Save and close the file.

5. Return to the Site Editor window and double-click index.htm to see how the modified navigation page now looks (**Figure 15**).

When you click your navigational links in Home Page, a new window opens with the assigned files. To test how the frames really work, you have to preview your page in a frames-compliant browser, such as any of the recent versions of Internet Explorer and Netscape Navigator.

To test the navigational frames layout:

1. Choose Preview in Browser from the Window menu and select one or both browsers from the submenu. Home Page automatically saves your file, and the frameset page opens in your browser(s).

2. Click all your links, making sure that each one links to the proper file (**Figure 16**).

✔ Tips

■ You can mix horizontal and vertical frames in your layout (**Figure 17**).

■ If you don't see the layout you're looking for in the Frame Assistant's Frame Layout screen, you can resize and add framesets to the layouts shown.

■ To delete a frame from a frameset, select that frame and press `Backspace` (Windows), or `Delete` (Mac). The HTML file will still be intact, but the frame will be deleted.

■ You can rearrange the position of frames on the page by using simply dragging the frame you want to move to a new location within the page.

Figure 16 Check the links by clicking each one and making sure the correct pages open.

Figure 17. This page contains a mix of horizontal and vertical frames. A static image sits at the top of the page above a vertical content frame and a vertical navigational frame.

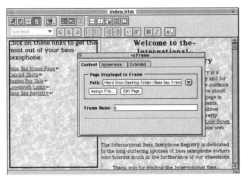

Figure 18. When you double-click on the frame you want to resize, the Frame Object Editor automatically opens with the information of the source file and the frame name in place.

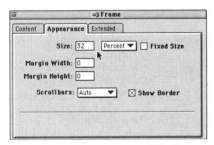

Figure 19. The Appearance tab of the Frame Object Editor offers a number of ways to revise the attributes of a frame.

Figure 20. Even if you resize a frame manually, you still may want to change its type of measurement in the Frame Object Editor's Appearance tab to either a percentage of the browser window, or to a fixed size.

Changing Frame Attributes

Frames can be changed in a number of ways using the Frame Object Editor. Or, if you simply want to change the size of a frame window, you can do so using your mouse.

To change the attributes of a frame:

1. Double-click a frame to open the Frame Object Editor (**Figure 18**).

2. Select the Appearance tab (**Figure 19**).

3. Change any of the frame attributes outlined in **Table 1** by selecting and entering new values.

To resize a frame manually:

1. Select the frame to be resized.

2. Click and hold a frame border with the mouse button (**Figure 20**).

3. Drag the border to its new position, and release the mouse.

Table 1.
Frame Object Editor: The Appearance tab

ELEMENT	WHAT IT DOES
Size	Allows you to express size as a fixed number of pixels, a percentage of the browser window, or stars, meaning the space left over—a "wild card" number.
Fixed Size	Limits the browser's ability to resize a frame (when checked).
Margin Width	Changes the indentation from the left-hand and right-hand margins. The default is zero, and the number is expressed in pixels.
Margin Height	Changes the indentation from the left top and bottom margins. The default is zero, and the number is expressed in pixels.
Scrollbars	Determine if a frame's scrollbars are automatically deployed as needed, always present, or never displays.
Show Border	Determines whether or not the selected frame bar appears as a visible border.

Advanced Frame Features

After you've created your frame-based page, you can use a suite of buttons and menu commands to do things like subdivide frames, add new ones, and reassign Root and Parent framesets (**Figure 21**). This is fairly easy to do, but because frames can be such a bane to some browsers, it's better to keep your framesets simple. **Table 2** gives you an idea of what these advanced features are. If you want to know more about advanced frame features, there's more information on the Home Page Visual Quickstart Guide Web site, at http://www.bigtent.com/chp3.

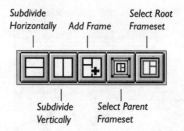

Figure 21. In Frame mode, there are five buttons added to the toolbar to use specifically for adding frames and working with existing frames layouts.

Table 2. The additional buttons of the Frame mode toolbar

BUTTON	WHAT IT DOES
Subdivide Horizontally	Divides a selected frame evenly into two horizontal frames.
Subdivide Vertically	Divides a selected frame evenly into two vertical frames.
Add Frame	Adds a Web page to the selected frame and divides the frame into two equal frames at the orientation of the original.
Select Parent Frameset	Selects the original frame and its "offspring" for making changes on all these frames.
Select Root Frameset	Selects all of the frames on the page, including all parent framesets.

Figure 22. When you change from Frames mode to Edit mode, Home Page displays the text message that users of non-compliant browsers will see.

Figure 23. Once you've changed the text, you can add a link to an alternative set of pages using the techniques shown in Chapter 5.

Providing for Non–Frames-Compliant Browsers

Even these days, some browsers or browser versions out there don't support frames. When such a browser tries to access a frame-based page, they display a message telling users that they cannot view the site. You can, however, offer an alternate point of entry to your site from this message to accommodate these users. If your home page uses hyperlinks in its text, you can send your noncompliant visitors there to give them access to your pages. However, if you are relying only on frames navigation, you may have to write an alternate, "no frames" home page.

To customize entry for non–frames-compliant browsers:

1. Open your frames page (index.htm, if you used the Frames Assistant).

2. Click the Edit Page mode button to switch to Edit mode. The text shows what users with non-compliant browsers see when they come to your site (**Figure 22**).

3. Select the second sentence (**Figure 23**), and compose a message that can serve as a link to your alternate home page.

Now you need to add the link to the new alternate home page.

To link to a new home page:

1. Select the text you want to use for the link.

2. Click the Link Editor button and select the target file from the file list or from the list of recent URLs in the Link Editor submenu.

✔ Tip

■ Testing this link is possible only if you have a non-compliant browser installed on your system.

SITE MANAGEMENT

```
┌─────────────────────────────────────────────┐
│ ▤▤▤         Site Editor - bass sax        ▤▤ │
├─────────────────────────────────────────────┤
│ ▢  ▢▢  ▢▣  ▣▣▣                               │
│ Local Site Folder: Hard Disk:Desktop Folder:bass sax: │
│ FTP Upload Location:                          │
├────────────────────┬──────┬──────────┬───────┤
│ Name               │ Size │Create Date│Last Mod Date│
├────────────────────┼──────┼──────────┼───────┤
│ 📁 bass sax         │  -   │Fri, Jan 2…│Sun, Feb 1…│
│   📄 bass-sax.html  │ 3 KB │Sun, Jan 1…│Mon, Feb 9…│
│   📄 basssaxregistry.html│1 KB│Sat, Jan 1…│Sun, Feb 1…│
│   📄 bs-template.html│1 KB │Fri, Jan 2…│Fri, Jan 23…│
│   📄 candids.html   │ 1 KB │Sun, Jan 1…│Mon, Feb 9…│
│   📄 forsale.html   │ 1 KB │Sun, Jan 1…│Thu, Jan 2…│
│ ▷ 📁 images         │  -   │Thu, Jan 2…│Tue, Feb 3,…│
│   📄 lowdown.html   │688 b…│Tue, Jan 2…│Thu, Jan 2…│
│   📄 registry.html  │ 5 KB │Sun, Jan 1…│Thu, Jan 2…│
│   📄 registry_home.html│867 b…│Fri, Feb 6…│Mon, Feb 9…│
│   📄 site_definition.wst│745 b…│Fri, Jan 2…│Fri, Jan 23…│
└────────────────────┴──────┴──────────┴───────┘
```

Figure 1. The Site Editor makes the discipline of folder-within-a-folder management easy.

Long ago, when Web pages were created by brave men and women akin to the barn-storming pilots of the early days of aviation, building Web pages was an ordeal, but getting them to actually appear on the Internet was even tougher.

One of Home Page's great strengths is its ability to upload your files once your site is ready to "go live", and to keep your site updated as time marches on. All this is thanks to the excellent Site Editor. This chapter reviews some of the basics of site management and shows you how to use the Site Editor's features to make publishing your site on the Web a breeze.

✔ Tip

■ Site-management procedures are identical whether your Web site is on the Internet or on an intranet. An *intranet* is simply a Web site that is used within a closed, local network rather than published to the global Internet. If you are building an intranet, ask your system administrator for information about accessing the server folders where your files will reside.

SITE MANAGEMENT

About Site Management

The Site Editor helps you organize your site on your local computer and manage the site when it resides on a server. Some of the techniques involved here were covered earlier. Since they're important in this context, here are some tips to keep in mind.

✔ Tips

- URL and image references to other HTML and image files are always shown as absolute references in their display windows. In other words, the URL window displays the link's file name along with its directory path (**Figure 2**). As long as your files are in the right folders, relative file locations will be referenced, despite what it the windows say.

- HTML files go inside the site folder, and image and multimedia files go in separate folders inside the site folder.

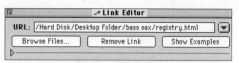

Figure 2. In the Link Editor, your links are displayed with addresses a mile long, starting with your hard drive, but when the files are uploaded, all the references will be relative to your site folder.

Figure 3. This is an HTML view of the page referenced in Figure 2. Note that the reference for "registry.html" is relative to the folder. In the third line above, note that the image reference is for a file within the images folder.

Good Web Practice

Mirroring

The key to good site management in Home Page—and to the advanced, easy-to-use features of the Site Editor—is to always have exact copies of your site on both the server and your hard drive. This arrangement is called *mirroring*.

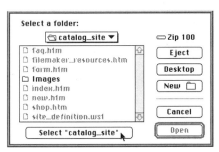

Figure 4. Choose an open folder and click Open "your site" (Windows), or Select "your site" (Mac).

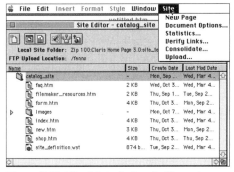

Figure 5. The Site Editor displays the files and folders that make up your site, and a new Site menu appears.

Table 1. The Site Editor toolbar buttons

BUTTON	WHAT IT DOES
Create New Page	Adds a new page to your site.
Document Options	Allows to you change different settings, such as link color and background images, in your pages.
Site Download Statistics	Describes how long a file or entire site will take to load to a server.
Verify Links and References	Verifies the links and references in your site.
Upload	Helps you upload your site to a server.
Consolidate	Moves all files connected to your site into your site folder.

Using the Site Editor

The Site Editor offers a number of tools that allow you to organize and check your site both on your local machine and on an external server.

The Site Editor also serves as a tool to upload your files easily, eliminating the need for an FTP client application to upload files. The

To open the Site Editor:

1. With Home Page open, choose Open Folder As Site from the File menu and from the dialog box that opens select the folder containing your site (**Figure 4**).

   or

   On your desktop, open the folder containing your site and double-click the icon labeled site_definition.wst.

   The Site Editor opens, displaying the contents of your site folder. A new Site menu appears as well (**Figure 5**).

✔ Tips

■ The Site Editor has its own toolbar (**Figure 6**). **Table 1** describes each of the tools and what they do.

■ The file extension .wst stands for Web site. The Site Editor uses this file to track the contents of your site.

Figure 6. The buttons in the Site Editor toolbar are the same as the options in the Site menu.

USING THE SITE EDITOR

Changing Document Options

Using the Site Editor, you can easily make a number of global changes to the appearance of your site. The Document Options feature gives you global control over background color, text and link colors, and background images (**Figure 7**). You can make changes on a file-by-file basis, or change all the pages in your site at once.

To change link colors throughout your site:

1. Choose Open Folder As Site from the File menu and in the dialog box that opens, select the folder containing your site.

2. Select an individual file in your site, or to change all your pages at once, select the site folder icon.

3. Click the Document Options button in the Site Editor toolbar, or select Document Options from the Site menu.

    The options dialog box appears with the Appearance tab selected. **Table 2** describes what each of its settings do.

4. Click and hold down the Normal Link button. A color palette appears (**Figure 8**).

5. Select a new color for your links and click OK.

✔ Tips

- If you have chosen to change an attribute your entire site, you will receive a warning that the links can't be returned to default colors once changed. To return the files to the default color, you must change files one by one.

- You can use this same procedure to change the background of your pages.

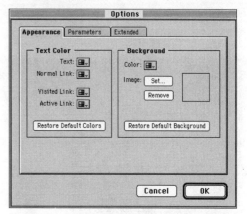

Figure 7. The Appearance tab of the Options dialog box allows you to change the links, text, and image background of a single file or your entire site.

Table 2. The Options dialog box: The Appearance tab

SETTING	WHAT IT DOES
Text	Changes the text color.
Normal Link	Changes the color of an unvisited link.
Visited Link	Changes the color of a visited link.
Active Link	Changes the color of a link when the user presses down on a link.
Background Color	Changes the background color.
Background Image	Sets or removes an image from the background of your page.

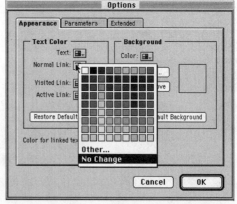

Figure 8. The Appearance tab allows you to change colors by choosing from a large color palette.

Figure 9. You can determine the download time of your site's HTML pages, image files, or multimedia files. HTML pages will include the download time for image and multimedia files associated with them.

Figure 10. The Site and Selection tabs indicate the total download time of your entire site and the download time of just the selected file.

Good Web Practice

Download Times

Generally speaking, any download time longer than 30 seconds is asking for your user's patience, which is the same as asking for trouble.

Checking Download Statistics

You may be wondering how all the kilobytes of data—images, audio, movie files—you're adding to your pages will affect your site's download time. The longer the download time, the more likely you are to lose visitors, so monitoring these document statistics is important.

To display download statistics using the Site Editor:

1. Choose Open Folder As Site in the dialog box that opens, select the folder containing your site.

2. Select the Site Download Statistics button from the Site Editor toolbar, or choose Statistics from the Site menu.

3. Select a file (**Figure 9**) and look at its statistics according to the approximate download time of six different Internet connection speeds (**Figure 10**).

4. Click Done when you're finished.

✔ Tip

■ The Statistics window is also useful when you have a limit to how many megabytes of data you can put on a server.

Verifying Links

When you publish your site on the Web, the last thing you want is a link that doesn't work. Avoid embarrassment and put the Site Editor's automatic links checking procedure on your pre-uploading to-do list.

To verify links:

1. With the Site Editor open, select the site folder or an individual file.

2. Click the Verify Links and References button on the toolbar, or choose Verify Links from the Site menu.

3. In the Verify dialog box, indicate whether you want to check the links on Selected Files/Folders or on the Entire Site, and click OK (**Figure 11**).

4. If one or more of your links doesn't work, use the Verify dialog box to fix the reference (**Figure 12**) by clicking the Browse Files button, locating the missing file, and clicking Change. You can use the Broken Link or Reference dialog box to change the link one occurrence at a time, or change every occurance of it at once by clicking Change All.

5. If you want to remove a link, select Remove Tag.

6. When you have fixed all problem references and verified all the pages, click OK in the Verification complete dialog box (**Figure 13**).

✔ Tip

■ If Home Page locates links to files outside the site folder, move the files inside the folder, redo the links, and reverify.

Figure 11. The Verify dialog box asks whether you want to check links on the entire site or on selected files and folders.

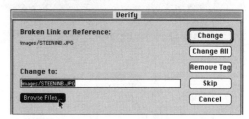

Figure 12. The Verify dialog box helps you fix broken links or references. Click Browse Files to find the file.

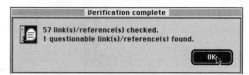

Figure 13. The verification complete dialog box tells you how many questionable links were found.

Figure 14.
The Consolidate dialog box lets you choose to consolidate the entire site, or just selected files or folders.

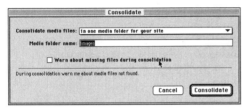

Figure 15. In the next Consolidate dialog box, choose in one media folder for your site. Name that folder in the Media Folder window.

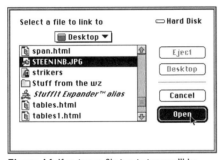

Figure 16. If an image file is missing, you'll be asked to locate it. Select the file and click Open, and the file is copied to the correct folder.

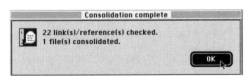

Figure 17. When one or more errant files have been consolidated into the correct media folder, this Consolidation complete message appears.

Consolidating Site Files

Your images and multimedia files need to be tucked nicely inside your site folder, preferably in their own folders. If your files are spread all over your hard drive, the Consolidate procedure helps you track them down and copy them into a single folder.

To consolidate all your site files:

1. Open your site in the Site Editor and select the site folder.

2. Click the Consolidate button on the toolbar or choose Consolidate from the Site menu.

3. In the Consolidate dialog box, select to either consolidate Selected Files/Folders or the Entire Site, and click OK (**Figure 14**).

4. Choose to consolidate media files in one media folder for your site, called *images* (or whatever you choose) (**Figure 15**). Select the check box if you want to be warned about missing files during the process of consolidation. Click Consolidate.

5. The program checks all the references in the folder. If there are missing files or references, a warning dialog box asks you to locate them (**Figure 16**). Home Page then copies the files into your site's folder.

6. When all the files are accounted for, the Consolidation Complete message appears, telling you how many references were checked and how many files were consolidated into the specified images folder (**Figure 17**). Click OK.

Preparing to Upload

When all your files and folders are finished, consolidated, and checked, it's time to upload your site to a server so people can access it via the World Wide Web. You only need to specify your Web server's location once. Home Page stores that information so you can update the site as your content changes.

To specify the upload server:

1. Open the Site Editor, and click the Upload button on the toolbar, or choose Upload from the Site Menu.

2. The Upload Location window opens (**Figure 18**). Click Set FTP Options to open the FTP Options window (**Figure 19**).

3. Enter the name of the Web server to which you will be uploading your files in the Server Name window.

4. Enter your user name in the User Name window.

5. Enter your password for uploading in the Password window (often your e-mail password, but you'll need to check this with your Internet Service Provider).

6. Click the Save Password check box if you want Home Page to remember your password for subsequent sessions.

7. Enter the name of the posting folder you've been assigned in the Remote Folder window.

8. The Upload Location section of the Upload dialog box now displays the server name and the name of the remote folder that will contain your files.

   All the information required to place your files on the server has now been entered.

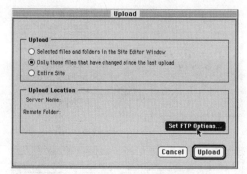

Figure 18. Click Set FTP Options in the Upload Location section of the Upload dialog box to begin the uploading process.

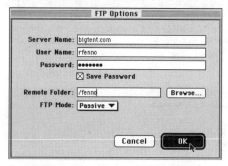

Figure 19. Unless you're worried about someone using your account, it's handy to check the Save Password check box and have the Site Editor store your password between sessions.

Good Web Practice
Uploading Files

To upload files, you need the following information from your Internet Service Provider, or system administrator:

- The name of your server.

- Your user name and account password.

- The name of the folder where your Web site will reside.

- Any guidelines for uploading, including any special file-naming conventions.

- What to call the default home page.

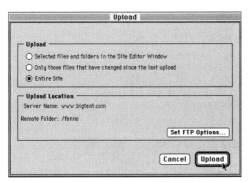

Figure 20. Check to see that the proper name and location of your server appear in the Upload location area. If not, repeat the steps in the previous section.

> **Uploading Site "bass sax"...**
> **(Press Command+Period to Cancel)**
> Press Cmd . to cancel

Figure 21. Once you access your Web server, your selected folder will begin uploading. You will see this message as files begin to transfer.

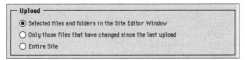

Figure 22. In the Upload section of the Upload window, click Selected files and folders in the Site Editor Window.

Uploading Your Site

Home Page provides for two kinds of uploading: initial uploading, which uploads your site files for the first time, and maintenance uploading, which updates files that have content that's changed since your last upload.

To upload files, you must first have completed the setup on the previous page. You must also have access to the Internet, either through a dial-up or network connection.

To upload a site to your server for the first time:

1. Open your site in the Site Editor, and click the Upload button on the toolbar or choose Upload from the Site Menu.

2. Select the Entire Site option and click the Upload button (**Figure 20**).

3. Your Internet dialer will connect you with the server you specified in the FTP Options and upload your files. Home Page tells you as the files are uploaded (**Figure 21**).

To upload selected files to your server:

1. Open your site in the Site Editor, and shift-click to select the files you want to upload.

2. Select the Selected files and folders option in the Site Editor Window (**Figure 22**) and click the Upload button.

3. Your Internet dialer will connect you with the server you specified in the FTP Options and upload the files you have selected.

To upload an open page to your server:

1. When a page you're working on is ready to be uploaded, choose Remote from the file menu, and choose Upload from the submenu (**Figure 23**).

2. A special Upload dialog box opens (**Figure 24**). Select the check box if you wish to include the image files associated with the page.

3. Check that the FTP settings are correct by clicking Set FTP Options.

4. When you return to the Upload dialog box, click Upload.

5. Your Internet dialer connects you with your server, and your file is uploaded.

✔ Tip

■ This technique is especially useful if you have a page that changes frequently, such as one that contains prices. When you upload the new version of the page onto your server, the new page file overwrites the old file.

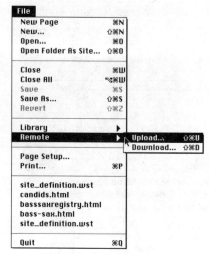

Figure 23. To upload an open file in Home Page, select Remote and Upload from the File menu.

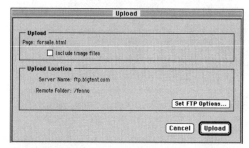

Figure 24. A special version of the Upload dialog box for an individual page uploads opens. Click the Include Image Files box to transfer images on the page. The FTP options should be the same as your site uploads. Clicking the Upload button opens the Internet connection and transfers the file.

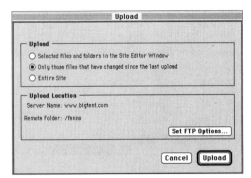

Figure 25. To update your site, click the Site Editor's Upload button, and select the option to upload only those files that have changed since the last upload. The Site Editor will upload only those files with more recent dates than the files on your server.

Updating Your Site

One of the great myths about the Web is that once you're up, your work is done. Timeliness is what people are looking for on the Web, and if your site is a constant source of timely information—whether selling your new, improved widgets or revealing which continent has the most bass saxophones—visitors will come back again and again.

Plan for updates on your site from the beginning, if only to clean up the inevitable typos that creep in.

To update your site:

1. Open your site in the Site Editor, and click the Upload button on the toolbar or choose Upload from the Site Menu.

2. In the Upload dialog box, select the option to upload only those files that have changed since the last upload (**Figure 25**).

3. Check to see that your FTP settings are correct by clicking the Set FTP Options button.

4. When you return to the Upload window, click the Upload button.

   Home Page will check the file dates of the site files on your hard drive against the dates on the server and replace any older versions on the server with the newer files from your hard drive.

Downloading and Deleting Files

Besides uploading, the other two things you will need to do with your server is download and delete files. The Site Editor has nothing to do with either of these actions—they happen from Home Page's File menu.

To download a file from a server to your hard drive:

1. Choose Remote from the File menu, then choose Download from the submenu (**Figure 26**).

2. The Download dialog box opens. Click the Change Download Options button (**Figure 27**) to open the Download Options dialog box.

3. The Download Options settings should match the Upload Options settings described in the Preparing to Upload section earlier in this chapter. If necessary, review that section to configure these settings.

4. Click the Browse button in the Download Options dialog box to open your Internet connection via the Browse FTP dialog box. Select the files you wish to download from the server (**Figure 28**).

5. In the Download location section of the Download dialog box, click the Browse button to select a folder where you want the downloaded files to be placed on your hard drive.

6. Click Download. Home Page downloads your files to the desired location.

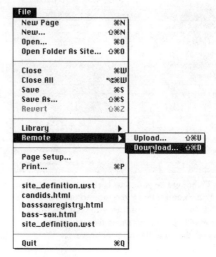

Figure 26. To download a file from the server, choose Remote and Download from the File menu.

Figure 27. When the Download dialog box opens, click the Change Download Options button.

Figure 28. Clicking Browse in the Download Options dialog box opens the Browse FTP dialog box, which connects you to the server and allows you to select from the files in the folder you've specified.

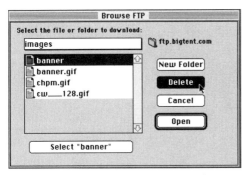

Figure 29. Find the file you wish to delete and click Delete.

Figure 30. Enter the new folder/directory name in the New Folder Name dialog box.

To delete files from your server:

1. Choose Remote from the File menu, then choose Download from the resulting submenu.

2. Click the Change Download Options button, opening the Download Options dialog box.

3. Click the Browse button. Your Internet dialer connects you with your server, and a Browse FTP dialog box opens, containing the files in your folder on the server.

4. Select the file you want to delete, and click Delete (**Figure 29**). A warning window asks if you are sure you want to delete the selected file. If you are, click Yes.

5. When you're through, click Cancel in the dialog boxes.

✔ Tips

■ You can also use the Browse FTP dialog box to place a new folder in your subdirectory on the server. Click the New Folder button and enter the name of the new folder in the dialog box that opens (**Figure 30**).

■ You can only delete one file at a time, because the Browse FTP window does not allow for multiple file selection.

DOWNLOADING AND DELETING FILES

123

FORMS

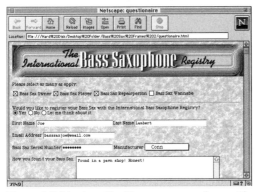

Figure 1. With a form like this one you can collect a wide range of information using a variety of text boxes, list boxes, and buttons.

The Web has text, images, and hyperlinks. But in its fullest flower it is also a highly interactive medium of audio, video, and even online virtual worlds. The interactivity created today will be laughable in the near future, as connections speed up and technologies continue to improve.

At present, however, Web designers have a limited number of tools with which to interact with users. Forms are one of them. Forms provide a method to collect information from visitors to your site, from simple questionnaires to sophisticated ordering systems. They then take this information and store it for you either in a file or in a database (**Figure 1**).

This chapter discusses forms—what they are and how to make them.

✔ Tip

- Forms are powered by a special scripting language called Common Gateway Interface (CGI). CGIs are task specific and must run on a server. Your Internet Service Provider (ISP) may have a library of CGIs for you. For this reason, consult with your ISP or system administrator about CGIs before you set out to make a page with forms.

Defining Form Areas

Forms are made up of form areas that contain objects such as buttons, text-entry areas, and drop-down list boxes your visitors will use to enter their data. You'll control the layout of the form area and its objects and can also include any sort of text and image elements in the form area. Once you've done this, you add the Submit button and the reference to the CGI's location on the server.

Before you create your forms, contact your ISP about the information you're going to process and ask for the appropriate CGI scripts.

To add a form area:

1. Open a Home Page document and place the insertion point on your page where you want the form area to appear.

2. Choose Form from the Insert menu and Form Area from the submenu (**Figure 2**). The form area appears and the form Object Editor opens.

3. In the Object Editor's Action window, enter the path of the CGI script you will be using for this form (**Figure 3**).

4. Select Post or Get from the Method list, depending on the information you get from your ISP (**Figure 4**).

5. Close the Object Editor. If you're working with an existing page, the form area now has the name of the script beneath the Home Page icon (**Figure 5**).

✔ Tips

- You can reopen the form's Object Editor by double-clicking anywhere in the form area, or by clicking the Object Editor button on the toolbar.

- The form area is expandable and will hold your forms items, along with any supporting text or images you include.

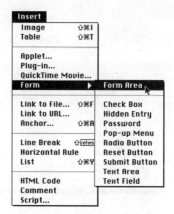

Figure 2. The Form menu shows the various objects you can use in a form.

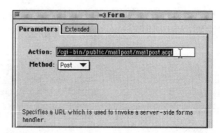

Figure 3. The Object Editor's Action Window. Unless you run your own server, you will need to ask your system administrator or ISP for the CGI pathname.

Figure 4. The Method list. Here, too, consult your system administrator or ISP for the proper setting.

Figure 5. The form area appears with the name of the script beneath the Home Page icon.

Figure 6. This page shows a number of the different form elements.

Table I. Form objects

FORM OBJECT	WHAT IT DOES
Check Box	Used to select one or more items in a list, or as a simple way of making a request.
Radio Button	Used to select only one item in a group.
Text Field	Used for posting one line of text at a time.
Text Area	Allows user to enter many lines of text; appears with scrollbars.
Scrolling List	Contains several options from which to choose by means of scrollbars. You can set the list to have just one or several choices.
Password Field	Used to enter data that is shown as bullets as it is entered.
Submit Buttons	Take the data entered in the form area and post it to the server's CGI for processing.
Reset	Clears all the fields in the form area.
Hidden	Keeps non-changing data in a place that the CGI uses to process its data.

Check *Radio* *Submit* *Reset*
box *button* *button* *button*

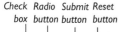

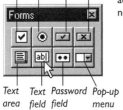

Text *Text* *Password* *Pop-up*
area *field* *field* *menu*

Figure 7. The forms palette gives you instant access to all the tools you need to create forms.

About Form Objects

Home Page enables you to add several objects to your form area (**Figure 6**). Each of these objects has its own purpose, and each has its own unique features that affect both your design and the way your CGI processes your data. **Table 1** describes these objects.

The Forms Palette (**Figure 7**) is the primary way of adding objects to your forms.

To open the Forms Palette:

Choose Forms Palette from the View menu (Windows) or Show Forms Palette from the Window menu (Mac).

✔ Tips

■ All form objects are also available by choosing Form from the Insert menu and then selecting the item from the resulting submenu. Or, you can keep the Forms palette open throughout your work session and select the objects from there.

■ Make sure that the Name and Value fields of the form objects are set to the requirements of your CGI script and any target application.

■ If there's any question in your mind about what to enter in the Action window of the Object Editor, or how to set up your form to work with the CGI script, consult your system administrator or Internet Service Provider.

ABOUT FORM OBJECTS

Adding Check Boxes

A check box allows your visitors to select
one or more items from a list within the
form area.

To add a check box to the form area:

1. In the form area, place the insertion point
   where you want a check box to appear.

2. Click the check box icon on the Forms
   palette (**Figure 8**) or choose Form from
   the Insert menu, then Check Box from the
   submenu. A check box appears at the
   insertion point (**Figure 9**), and the Check
   Box Object Editor opens.

3. Enter a name for the check box conform-
   ing to the CGI information you've
   obtained from your ISP in the Name window, and enter text in the Value window
   to describe the information the check box
   represents (**Figure 10**). If you select
   Checked, the check box will be checked
   by default.

4. Close the Object Editor, place the insertion
   point to the right of the check box, and
   enter text telling your users what the
   check box represents on your page.

5. Continue adding check boxes for all the
   items on your list by repeating Steps 2–4
   (**Figure 11**).

✔ Tip

■ To more accurately align objects, you can
   place them in tables in your form area.
   Just place the insertion point inside the
   form area, then choose Table from the
   Insert menu, and add your form objects to
   the table cells.

Figure 8. Keep the Forms
palette open during your
work session for easy access.

Figure 9. The Check Box Object Editor opens
automatically when you place a check box in the form.

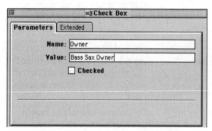

Figure 10. The name you place in your Name
window should conform to CGI posting
requirements.

Figure 11. Add names for your check boxes directly
on the page after you enter the values in the Check
Box Object Editor.

Figure 12. The Radio Button Object Editor automatically generates a name and value for your button, which you can change.

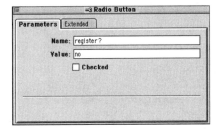

Figure 13. All the radio buttons in a group must have the same name.

Figure 14. If you can check more than one radio button, go back to the Object Editor to make sure that the Name fields for all the radio buttons are identical.

Adding Radio Buttons

Just like the buttons on an old radio, a group of radio buttons allows only one button to be selected at a time. Radio buttons are often used in sets of two, for yes-no or true-false selection. In creating them, you must group radio buttons together by assigning them all the same name in the Object Editor. You then differentiate between them by assigning a unique value to each button and by labeling them with different text on your page.

To add a radio button to a form area:

1. Place the insertion point where you want the radio buttons to be.

2. From the Insert menu, choose Form and Radio Button, or click the Radio Button button on the Forms palette. A radio button appears, and the Radio Button Object Editor opens (**Figure 12**).

3. In the Object Editor's Name window, enter the name for the radio button according to the CGI instructions from your Internet Service Provider. In the Value field, enter the condition that the button describes (**Figure 13**). Close the Object Editor.

4. Place the insertion point next to the radio button and add text next to it that describes the button.

5. Repeat steps 1–4 above to add more buttons, using the same name, but different values and text descriptions, for all of them.

6. Close the Object Editor.

✔ Tip

■ Check the radio buttons by selecting them and making sure you can't select more than one button in a set at a time (**Figure 14**).

Adding Text-Entry Objects

Three different types of text objects are used to collect input in a form area, as described in Table 2.

To add a text-entry object to a form area:

1. Place the insertion point where you want the text-entry object to appear.

2. Choose Form from the Insert menu and the type of text-entry object you want to insert, or use one of the buttons on the Forms palette. The selected text-entry object appears at the insertion point, and its Object Editor opens.

3. Enter the name you will be using for this text in the Name window according to the CGI instructions from your ISP (**Figure 15**).

4. Designate the size of your text object by entering a new number in the Size window, or by clicking and dragging the selected objects.

5. Repeat steps 1–4 for each text-entry object you want to add to the form area (**Figure 16**).

✔ Tips

■ The Text Area object's Object Editor also has windows for specifying Rows and Columns within the area, and a drop-down list showing how the area will handle word wrap.

■ Add default text to a text object to guide the user into using standard data formats. For example, by entering *account@domain* in a field for collecting e-mail addresses, you may cut down on user entry errors.

Table 2. Form Text objects

OBJECT	WHAT IT DOES
Text Fields	Collect short lines of text.
Text Areas	Collect lengthy text input.
Password	Used to enter single lines of text that appear on the user's screen as bullets or asterisks.

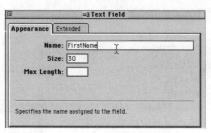

Figure 15. Notice that you can establish the size of the text area in the Object Editor, something you can also do by dragging the area with your mouse.

Figure 16. This example contains all the different kinds of text fields, areas and passwords.

Figure 17. Scrolling lists both make your forms easier to fill out and keep the information you collect more consistent.

Figure 18. If you want an item to be selected by default, select it in the Check column.

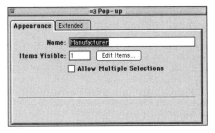

Figure 19. The Pop-up Object Editor lets you control how many items in your list will appear and whether the user can make multiple selections.

Pop-up Menus and Scrolling Lists

A pop-up menu or scrolling list allows you to offer users a predetermined list of form items to choose from, making your form more manageable both of you. Not only does this object make it easier to fill out your form, but since the user can only choose what you've offered, it ensures that you will collect consistent information (**Figure 17**).

To create a pop-up menu or scrolling list:

1. Place the insertion point where you want to place the list of items.

2. From the Insert menu, choose Form, then Pop-up Menu, or click the Pop-up Menu button on the Forms palette, and enter a descriptive name for your list in the Name field (**Figure 19**).

3. In the Items Visible field, enter 1 if you want the object to be a pop-up menu, or enter a number greater than one (2-100) if you want the object to be a scrolling list.

4. Click Edit Items to open the Define Pop-up List window.

5. Under Title, double-click the first item to select it, and enter a name for the first item for your list. Then double-click the *Value* and enter a condition that corresponds to the title according to the CGI instructions from your ISP.

6. Click the Add button and repeat the process until you have built your whole list (**Figure 18**).

7. Click OK to return to the Object Editor.

8. In the Items Visible window, select the number of items you want to display.

9. Close the Object Editor and make sure your list appears as you want it to.

Adding Hidden Form Objects

When you are setting up your page to work with a CGI script, you may need to use hidden fields. These objects are usually used to supply information that isn't based on user input to a CGI script, and your systems administrator or ISP will let you know when they're required. When viewers submit their forms, the hidden data is sent to the server along with the data they have entered in the form. True to their name, hidden fields are not visible on a browser.

To add a hidden-form object to a form area:

1. Place the insertion point anywhere in the form area. You can place hidden form objects anywhere.

2. Choose Form from the Insert menu, then choose Hidden Entry from the resulting submenu. In Edit mode, a place-keeper for the hidden object appears, and the Hidden Form Entry Object Editor opens (**Figure 20**).

3. Fill in the windows for Entry Name and Entry Value according to the requirements of your CGI script.

4. Close the Object Editor.

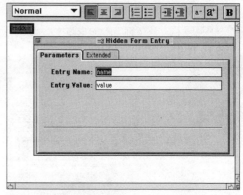

Figure 20. Hidden entries store information that your users don't need to see but that your CGI scripts need to function properly.

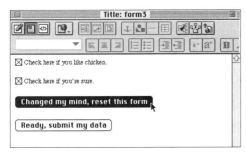

Figure 21. Reset buttons are like Undo, they give users a chance to change their minds.

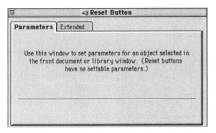

Figure 22. Reset buttons have no settable parameters because this button does only one thing: reset the entries in the Forms Area.

Figure 23. You can edit the text on a Reset button to fit the tone and style of your form.

Adding a Reset Button

A Reset button's purpose is to clear all the entries within a form area so that the user can change the data they've fill out in your form. Reset buttons often sit next to the Submit button. They are the only form object that does not rely on CGI to work (**Figure 21**).

To add a Reset button to the form area:

1. Place the insertion point where you want the Reset button to be.

2. From the Insert menu, choose Form and then Reset Button or click the Reset button's button on the Forms palette.

3. The Reset button appears at the insertion point, and its Object Editor opens, informing you that there are no settable parameters for Reset buttons (**Figure 22**). Close button the Object Editor.

4. You can change the Reset button's name by double-clicking the default text and then typing over it (**Figure 23**).

Adding a Submit Button

The Submit button sends the information entered into the forms area to the CGI script for processing (**Figure 24**).

You can modify a Submit button's appearance by either changing the text that appears on the button, or replacing the button altogether with an image of your own.

To add a Submit button to a form area:

1. Place the insertion point where you want the Submit button to be on your page.

2. Choose Form from the Insert menu and the Submit Button, or click the Submit button on the Forms palette. The Submit button Object Editor appears.

3. In the Action Name window of Object Editor, type the name of the action your CGI script requires (**Figure 25**).

4. Close the Object Editor and change the button text if you want to by double-clicking the button text and typing over it.

✔ Tip

■ Although multiple Submit buttons can handle different tasks, stick with one submit button per form area unless you fully understand how CGI works.

Figure 24. After users fill out your form, they'll need to submit it so you can process the data.

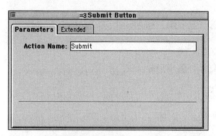

Figure 25. You can name your button in the Object Editor, or just double-click it on your page and overwrite the default text.

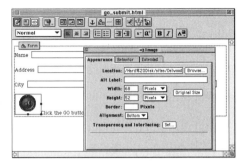

Figure 26. You can brighten up your web page by using an image instead of a standard submit button.

Figure 27. The Image Object Editor lets you designate an image as a Submit button.

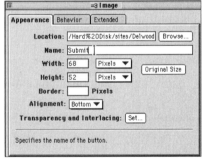

Figure 28. It's helpful if you choose a name for your image that reminds you what it's for, like *Submit*.

To use an image as a submit button:

1. Place the image on your page that will serve as your Submit button, and double-click it to open the image's Object Editor (**Figure 26**).

2. Click the Behavior tab, and choose Form Submit Button from the Behavior list (**Figure 27**).

3. Click the Appearance tab. In the Name window, enter the action of the button, generally Submit (**Figure 28**).

4. Close the Object Editor.

✔ Tips

- Because Submit buttons work with scripts residing on your server, you will not be able to test their functionality without being connected to the internet using your browser.

- Not all browsers can handle multiple Submit buttons.

- Be absolutely certain you meet your CGI script's requirements with your Submit button. The quality of the data you collect depends on it.

USING AN IMAGE AS A SUBMIT BUTTON

CONNECTING TO FILEMAKER PRO

Figure 1. FileMaker Pro is a powerful, easy-to-use relational database available for Windows and Mac systems. With a dedicated server, you can develop a system that can integrate FileMaker Pro with Home Page to put your database on the Web.

Of all its tricks and talents, nothing Home Page does compares to its newly added linkage with FileMaker Pro 4.0.

By linking FileMaker Pro to Home Page, you can create sites that serve content to your Web pages dynamically. A database containing anything from store inventory, to your top ten list of the day, to all the poetry you wrote in high school can be served to the Web. Visitors benefit from greater interactivity that lets them search and add to your site, and you benefit from much easier ways of generating pages and managing content.

Home Page comes with the useful FileMaker Pro Connection Assistant, which helps you connect to a database step by step. This chapter shows you how to use this Assistant.

Important: To publish a FileMaker database, FileMaker Pro 4 must be running on a Web server with the database file open. You either have to dedicate a server with a full-time connection to the Internet, or contact FileMaker, Inc. for a list of several Internet Service Providers offering this special hosting service.

✔ Tip

- For more information about using FileMaker Pro on the Internet, see *Database Publishing with FileMaker Pro on the Web,* by Maria Langer (Peachpit Press, ©1998).

About FileMaker Pro

This chapter assumes you are familiar with FileMaker Pro 4.0 and its terminology. You should know that FileMaker organizes information in records, which are made up of fields. The records and fields are displayed using layouts (**Figure 2**). **Table 1** defines these terms.

FileMaker Pro 4.0 provides two ways to publish a database on the Internet:

♦ *Instant Web Publishing* publishes a database directly to the Internet with an interface similar to FileMaker's. This offers users with password-controlled access the ability to view, add, edit, delete, search, and sort records.

♦ *Custom Web Publishing* uses both HTML and CDML (Claris Dynamic Markup Language) tags to build files that present more complex dynamic pages to the Web.

Home Page's FileMaker Pro Assistant enables you to perform Custom Web Publishing functions without having to learn HTML or CDML. Intrepid Web publishers choose a more freewheeling approach by using two other FileMaker Connection features: the FileMaker Form Library and the FileMaker Reference Library. With them, tagging in CDML is a point-and-click process.

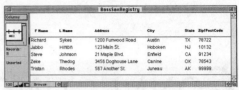

Figure 2. This FileMaker Pro database displays a group of records in a column layout. Each line contains a record, which is made of a collection of fields, such as first name, last name, and address.

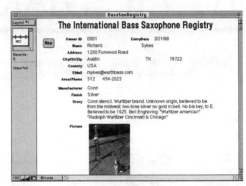

Figure 3. In this layout, the same information from Figure 2 is displayed one record at a time. Each line of information has its own screen. This screen was designed for entering new records. Note the New button, which opens a new record for entry when clicked.

Figure 4. Another layout doesn't display all of the record's fields. Layouts are often customized so that only the fields required for a class of user are displayed.

Table 1. The units of a FileMaker database

TERM	WHAT IT IS
field	The basic unit of a database file. Fields store, display and sometimes calculate data.
record	A group of fields.
layout	A defined way of displaying records from the database.

Figure 5. Place your database file inside the Web folder, which is inside the FileMaker Pro folder.

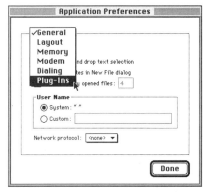

Figure 6. Choose plug-ins from the list of Application Preferences options.

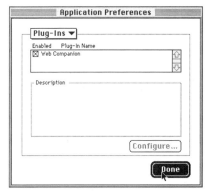

Figure 7. Select the check box next to Web Companion.

Preparing a FileMaker Database

Although it's possible to publish an "empty" database on the Web and allow visitors to fill it with records, more likely you'll want to display an existing FileMaker database on the Web. After you design your database and populate it with records, there are a few simple steps you need to follow to prepare it for use with Home Page.

To prepare a FileMaker database for Home Page:

1. When your FileMaker database is ready, make sure it's saved in the Web folder inside your FileMaker Pro 4.0 Folder (**Figure 5**).

2. In FileMaker, choose Preferences from the Edit menu, then choose Application from the submenu. The Application Preferences window appears. You must be connected to the Internet to complete these steps.

3. Choose Plug-Ins from the list (**Figure 6**), select the Web Companion check box, then click Done (**Figure 7**).

4. Open the database you wish to publish in FileMaker.

5. Choose Sharing from the File menu. In the File Sharing window, select the Web Companion check box, and click OK.

Your database is now ready for Home Page's FileMaker Connection Assistant.

The FileMaker Connection Assistant

The FileMaker Connection Assistant walks you through the process of building all the pages that will present your FileMaker Pro database online.

The assistant builds pages that allow your visitor to search your database, view and manipulate individual records by editing, deleting, or duplicating them, and add new records.

To open the FileMaker Connection Assistant:

1. Open your database in FileMaker Pro.

2. Open Home Page.

3. In Home Page, choose New from the File menu (**Figure 8**).

4. In the New window, click the Use Assistant button, select FileMaker Connection Assistant from the list (**Figure 9**), and click OK. The FileMaker Connection Assistant opens with the Overview page.

5. Read the Overview (**Figure 10**) to learn more about the FileMaker Connection Assistant, then click Next.

Figure 8. With your database open in FileMaker, launch Home Page and choose New from the File Menu.

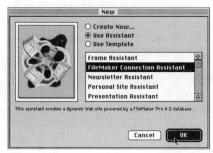

Figure 9. When the New window opens, click Use Assistant, and select FileMaker Connection Assistant from the list of assistants.

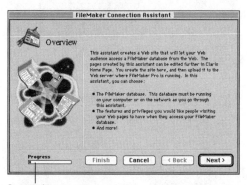

Progress bar

Figure 10. The Overview page explains more about the FileMaker Connection Assistant. Note the progress bar in the lower-left corner, which tells you how far along you are toward completing your project.

Figure 11. The Before You Begin window explains how FileMaker works as a Web server, as well as several items of interest about TCP/IP connection and file security.

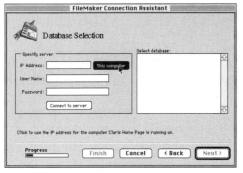

Figure 12. Either insert an IP address for the computer running FileMaker Pro or click the button marked *This Computer* to use the system you are working on.

Figure 13. You only need to enter a user name and password if your FileMaker database requires them.

Figure 14. Select the databases you will use to build Web pages.

Selecting a Database

In order to produce a set of Web pages that access your database, you must declare the location of a running copy of FileMaker Pro in Home Page. This copy must be running permanently, and you'll need its TCP/IP identification. You can get this number from your systems administrator; or if you are setting up a server on the same system on which you are doing your work, you can use that computer's TCP/IP address. You must be running TCP/IP software on whatever computer you are using to run FileMaker Pro.

To select the database:

1. Still in the assistant, the next step is to review the Before You Begin window (**Figure 11**). Read these paragraphs, then click Next.

    The Database Selection screen appears.

2. In the IP Address text box, enter the IP address of the system that is running FileMaker, or click the This Computer button to select the system you are using (**Figure 12**).

3. Enter your User Name and Password if the system running FileMaker requires password access, then click the Connect to Server button (**Figure 13**). A list of databases appears.

4. Choose the database you will use to build your system (**Figure 14**), and click Next.

    The Layout Selection page appears.

Selecting a Layout

FileMaker Pro uses layouts to display different combinations of information from a database. In the Layout Selection window, you choose a FileMaker layout that contains all the fields you want to display on the Web.

To choose a FileMaker Pro layout:

1. Read the explanation about why you need to choose a layout in the Layout Selection screen.

2. Choose a layout from the drop-down list, which contains the fields you'll need on the Web (**Figure 15**), then click Next.

✔ Tips

- You can select a layout with more fields than you plan to display on the Web, though this will decrease performance of your site.

- If your FileMaker database has only one layout and it contains every field in your database, click the Cancel button and make a special layout containing just the fields you'll need for Web use. Then start over by returning to Home Page and choosing New from the File menu to reopen the FileMaker Connection Assistant.

Figure 15. Select a layout from the drop-down list for use in building Web pages. The fewer unused fields you have in the selected layout, the better your site will perform.

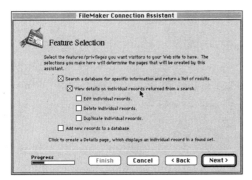

Figure 16. In this example, a system will be developed that allows the Web user to search for information in list form, as well as display individual records that meet the criteria of the search.

Selecting Database Features

The Feature Selection screen establishes how Web visitors will see your database on the Web. How much control will they have over your data? Will they be able to edit records? Delete records? Add records to the database? These are the issues you settle here.

The choices you make in the Feature Selection screen determine which of the remaining screens in the FileMaker Connection Assistant you will see. If you choose to make your data searchable, the FileMaker Connection Assistant will lead you through a number of additional screens to create the different components of a search page. Similarly, if you allow the user to add records to your database, the assistant will provide you a page to create that entry screen.

To select features:

1. Read the Feature Selection screen.

2. Click the buttons corresponding to how much user access and interaction you want to allow (**Figure 16**). Explanations for the function of each feature appear when you place your cursor over each of the items in the window.

3. Click Next.

Setting Search Page Options

If you choose to allow your visitor to search your database, the FileMaker Connection Assistant will lead you through a number of screens to create a search page, a search results page, and a details page. A *search page* allows your user to *query* your database, or ask which records contain certain information. A search produces a *search results page* that contains all of the records that meet the criteria of the visitor's search. Each of the records can then be viewed in greater detail on a *details page*. In the following screens, you determine the parameters of the search, search results, and details pages.

The Search Page screen helps you determine which fields the user can search on, if any. A *canned search* requires no input from the user. This is useful, for example, if you simply want to display information from a specific date in a schedule.

In building your search pages, you program the logic of the search by choosing operators. *Operators* are logical statements that determine the relationships of different fields (**Table 2**).

To set search options:

1. From the list of fields on the left side of the window, choose a field you want users to be able to search, and then click the Add button to add the field to the Search Page Fields window (**Figure 17**). Repeat this action until the list contains all the search fields you want to use on your search page.

2. For each of the fields, change the label in the Field label window to reflect the field name you'd like users to see (**Figure 18**).

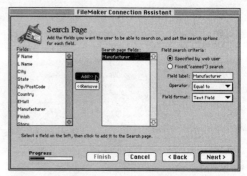

Figure 17. In this example, *Specified by Web user* is checked, allowing the visitor to search your site using criteria they choose.

Figure 18. The label of a search field allows you to change what the user will see, for example, *Made by* instead of *Manufacturer*. This can be useful, because databases often have fields that have names in shorthand.

Table 2. Search Page operators

OPERATOR	WHAT IT DOES
Equal to	Determines records that match the search criteria exactly.
Not equal to	Determines which records do not match the search criteria.
Less than	Determines records whose numerical value is less than the search criteria value.
Less than or equal to	Determines records whose values are less than or exactly equal to the search criteria.
Greater than	Determines records whose values are greater than the search criteria.
Greater than or equal to	Determines records whose values are greater than or exactly equal to the search criteria.
Contains	Determines records that contain the character or string of characters in the search criteria.
Begins with	Determines records that begin with the character or string of characters specified in the search criteria.
Ends with	Determines records that end with the character or string of characters specified in the search criteria.

Figure 19. Pop-up menus can correspond with pop-up menu lists in FileMaker Pro. Set the number of records visible when the list is inactive and select Multiple selections if you want the user to be able to choose more than one item from the list.

3. Choose whether the search will be Specified by Web user or a Fixed ("canned") search.

4. Select the operator for each field from the Operator window.

5. Select the format of the search results.

6. When you've set up all of the search criteria, click Next.

If you have selected a field value that requires a list, insert the name of the value list in the Value list window. If you select a pop-up menu, enter the number of items visible and whether or not to allow multiple selections (Figure 19). When you are through with these settings, click Next.

✔ Tips

- If you are the least bit unclear about these steps, go through the FileMaker Pro tutorial installed with FileMaker.

- Field formats correspond to the formats that you used in designing your database. If the field format is text, text area, image, or read-only text, there will be no values list because no values need to be defined.

- A search page can have either a positive or negative outcome, so the Assistant builds a page that displays the records meeting a set of search criteria, as well as a page that displays a negative result when no matching records are found.

Setting Search Page Logical Operators

If you create more than one search field in the Search Page Options screen, you need to determine their relationships to the search in the Search Page Logical Operator screen.

For example, if your search page fields are *color* and *manufacturer*, you indicate in this window whether you'll be looking for red Oldsmobiles (*red and Oldsmobile*) or all cars that are red and all cars that are Oldsmobiles (*red or Oldsmobile*).

To set search page logical operators:

1. If you want to leave the choice of operators up to the user, click User Specified.

   or

   If you want to set logic to the search that will always be in place, then click the Fixed button.

2. If you choose a fixed search logic, choose either And or Or from the drop-down list (**Figure 20**). If you want all the search criteria to be met, choose And. If you want any of the search criteria to be met, choose Or.

3. Click Next.

Figure 20. The Search Page Logical Operator screen determines whether the user can look for records matching any search criterion selected or for records matching all of the criteria.

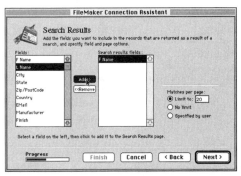

Figure 21. In the Search Results screen, add fields to be displayed when records of a search are shown. Select from the Fields list, then click Add to place the fields in the Search results fields list.

Figure 22. Decide how many records to display on a page. You can opt to set no limit to the number of records that display, or let the user choose how many records to view.

Setting Search Results Options

The FileMaker Pro Connection Assistant is all about setting up pages, and the most special of these pages is the one that contains search results.

In the Search Results screen, you determine what data is displayed in a search results page. Each record in a database has a number of fields of information, not all of which will be relevant for your search. If, for example, you set your search page to look for red Oldsmobiles, you may or may not want to display the name of the owner as well. This window is where you would choose to do so.

To set options for search results:

1. From the list on the left-hand window, select an item, and click the Add button to add it to the list on the right (**Figure 21**). Repeat this procedure until all the fields you want to display in your search page are present in the list on the right.

2. Set the number of records to be displayed on the search results page by setting limits under Matches per page (**Figure 22**).

3. If you select the Limit to: radio button, enter the number of matching records to display per page. The user will see as many as you choose. Home Page will create pages with More buttons at the bottom that link to pages displaying the additional records.

4. Click Next.

Setting Sort Options

Next you specify how the search results are to be sorted when they are displayed on the search results page.

To set sort options:

1. Select whether you want search results to be sorted (**Figure 23**).

   ♦ Click Yes and specify a predetermined sort order if you want the results of the search to be sorted before being displayed in the search results page. You will choose how to sort the results next.

   ♦ Click Yes and allow the visitor to select a field to sort with if you want the visitor to use a pop-up menu from which to select the sort field, along with ascending or descending sort selection.

   ♦ Click No Sort Order if you want the search results to be posted without being sorted.

   If you choose No Sort Order, you see the Details Page screen, which is on the following page. Otherwise, the Predetermined Sort Order screen appears. This is where you choose which of the results page fields will be used for sorting.

To set predetermined sort order:

1. Select a field from the Results Page Fields list.

2. Click the Add button.

3. Choose either Ascending or Descending order (**Figure 24**).

4. Choose another search field and its ascending or descending order if needed.

5. Click Next.

Figure 23. The Sort Results screen asks if you want to specify a sort order for your records.

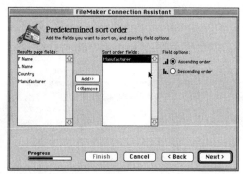

Figure 24. The Predetermined Sort Order screen asks you how the records are to be sorted. The results can be sorted by a specific field and displayed in ascending or descending order.

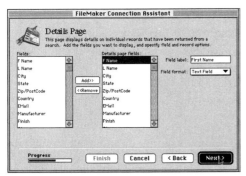

Figure 25. Select and click individual fields until you have a list of the fields needed for the Details Page.

Setting Detail Page Options

Now you create the details page. A details page appears when the link in the results page is clicked. It displays one record at a time from the database. The FileMaker Connection Assistant generates this link automatically.

To set options for a details page:

1. Select a field from the Fields list. Click Add, adding the field to the Details page fields list. Keep adding these items until you have a list of all the items you wish to appear on the details page.

2. Edit the name of each field in the Field label window. Users will see the description you enter here, so be descriptive.

3. Specify a format for each field as an HTML object from the Field Format list.

4. If you chose to allow editing access, set options for each item from the Values list box, the Items visible box, and the Multiple Selections check box.

5. When these settings are complete, click Next (**Figure 25**).

✔ Tip

■ Setting access privileges in the Feature Selection screen allows users to edit, delete, or duplicate records from details pages.

SETTING DETAIL PAGE OPTIONS

149

Setting New Record Page Options

If you chose to allow visitors to add to your database in the Feature Selection screen, you will now see the New Record Page screen. Here you specify options for adding new records to your database.

If you are not allowing users to enter records to your database, you will skip this New Records Page and see the Additional Pages screen instead.

To set options for the new record page:

1. From the Fields list, choose the field to be used in the new record page. Click the Add button to add the field to the New record fields list. Continue adding fields that you want on the new record page.

2. Edit the name of each field in the Field label window. The Field label is the description of a field that the user will see (**Figure 26**).

3. Specify a format for each field from the Field format list.

4. When these settings are complete, click Next.

About Additional Pages

The Additional Pages screen explains that the FileMaker Connection Assistant will generate additional reply and error pages based on the features you selected in the Assistant's previous windows (**Figure 27**).

To learn about additional pages:

1. Read the window.

2. Click Next when you are done.

Figure 26. The New Record Page builds a page for the user to add new records to the FileMaker Pro database. Add the field names to the New Record fields, and adjust the Field labels as needed. The screen only appears if you choose to allow users to add to your database in the Feature Selection screen.

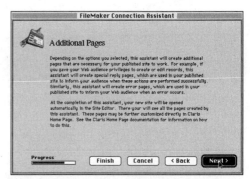

Figure 27. The Additional Pages screen explains how additional pages will be handled, depending upon the options you have selected.

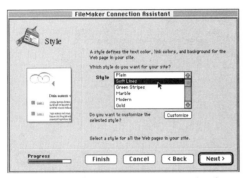

Figure 28. The Style screen allows you to select from several ready-made styles for your Web site. The window on the left shows you a preview of the style.

Figure 29. Click Customize to refine one of these styles.

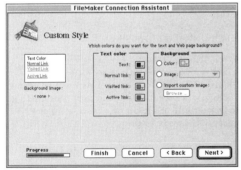

Figure 30. The Custom Style screen is where you can set text colors, set background color for the pages, or import an image as a background.

Selecting a Style

The Style screen gives you the option of selecting a ready-made page background with distinctive text styles. A preview window for each of the styles is displayed in the left side of the window.

To select a style:

1. Scroll through the list of ready-made styles (**Figure 28**).

2. When you decide on a style, click Next to continue to the next window. Home Page uses the highlighted style to generate your pages.

To change a layout:

1. Click the Customize button at the bottom of the Style list (**Figure 29**).

   The Custom Style screen appears (**Figure 30**).

2. Set the text link colors as well as background color and images according to your desires.

3. Click Next.

✔ Tip

■ You can also change the style of your site once you are through working with the FileMaker Connection Assistant using formatting, image placement, and other skills you learned in earlier chapters.

Choosing a Location

The Final Hints and Suggestions screen (**Figure 31**) offers information on where you should place your site. Read this screen and click Next. The Location Screen appears. You now must decide whether to generate your site into a new folder or in an existing one.

To set a location for new files:

1. Click New Folder to have the assistant create a new folder for the files it will create.

   or

   Click Existing Folder to have the files placed into an existing folder on your hard drive.

2. Use the resulting dialog box to name either the new site folder (**Figure 32**) or to identify the folder where you want the files to go.

   You return to the Location window, which now displays the added file location you have selected (**Figure 33**), along with more helpful advice about consolidating the image files in the Site Editor once the pages are generated.

3. Click Create. The FileMaker Connection Assistant makes your files.

✔ Tip

■ Heed the warning in the Location screen: writing the files to an existing folder could overwrite some existing files, especially if another assistant generated them. Usually, you'll want to place the files in a new folder.

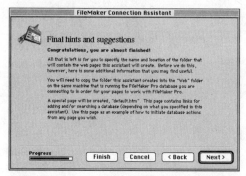

Figure 31. The Final Hints and Suggestions screen congratulated you and explains what's going to be happening when the pages are generated.

Figure 32. FileMaker Connection Assistant asks in the Location window if the files about to be generated are to be inserted into a folder that exists, or if a new folder will be made for them.

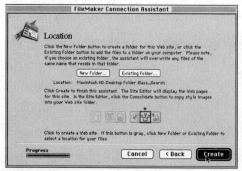

Figure 33. The Location screen offers useful information about consolidating your files.

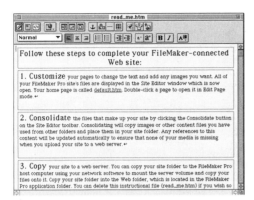

Figure 34. The Site Editor and a file called read_me.htm open when the site is complete. This page explains the remaining steps to going live on the Web.

Figure 35. Customize your files and then test them in your browser. Be sure your files are in the Web folder and that FileMaker Pro is correctly linked.

Generating the Working Site

The next screen you see is an HTML file called read_me.htm (**Figure 34**), which outlines the four steps required to make the FileMaker Connection Assistant files into a working Web site.

To complete your site:

1. Customize your pages so that they have a personalized look using the techniques described in the first three chapters. You can manage your files from the Site Editor in Edit mode.

2. Consolidate the image files you have used in the process of generating the pages using the techniques described in Chapter 9.

3. Copy the site to a Web server. Be sure you have FileMaker Pro 4 running on the server. Place the folder inside the Web folder, which is inside FileMaker Pro's application folder. Consult FileMaker Pro's documentation to make sure your file locations are correct.

4. Connect to your site for testing by using its IP address and the subfolder that has the location of the files. Test the links to the database (**Figure 35**).

✔ Tip

■ Taking you to this point should be just enough to whet your appetite. For more information about linking FileMaker Pro with Claris Home Page, read Chapter 10 in the PDF version of the Home Page user's guide.

GENERATING THE WORKING SITE

APPENDIX A:

APPLICATION OPTIONS/PREFERENCES

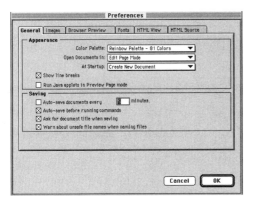

Figure 1. The General Tab, which is displayed when the Applications Options or Preferences item is chosen has sections controlling Appearance and Saving of files.

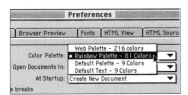

Figure 2. To increase the number of available colors, select the 216-color Web Palette from the Color Palette window.

Application Options in the Windows Tools menu and Preferences in the Macintosh Edit menu contain important settings that you can customize to meet your needs and tastes. There are six tabs in this window that control output options, the way your text and other page elements looks onscreen, and many other program settings.

General

The General tab (**Figure 1**) is split up into two section that allow you to control the appearance and behavior of your page at start up, and adjust saving options.

Color Palette

The Color Palette drop-down list (**Figure 2**) lets you specify the color palette you wish to use when constructing your Web pages. The default palette is *Rainbow Palette - 81 Colors*, which has (you guessed it) 81 very safe Web colors You can also expand your color range and select *Web Palette - 216 colors*, which would only cause problems on some early Windows machines. Want to make absolutely sure your colors will display properly? Then select one of the two 9-color palettes: *Default Palette - 9 Colors*, or *Default Text - 9 Colors*. You'll also be able to override color palettes by accessing the colors available on your system through your color picker.

Open Documents

This list (**Figure 3**) lets you select which mode Home Page will be in when you open your HTML or Home Page document pages. The default setting opens pages in Edit Page mode, the table below describes them all.

Figure 3. Select a mode to open in.

Table 1.
The Open Documents drop-down list

LIST ITEM	WHAT IT DOES
Edit Page Mode	Opens documents in Edit mode.
Preview Page Mode	Opens documents in Preview mode.

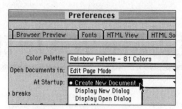

Figure 4. Select what happens when you launch Home Page.

At Startup

The At Startup list (**Figure 4**) specifies what Home Page does automatically after launching. The default setting is Creates New Document, the table below describes them all.

Table 2. The At Startup drop-down list

LIST ITEM	WHAT IT DOES
Create New Document	Opens a new document, called *untitled*.
Display New Dialog	Displays the New Dialog Box.
Display Open Dialog	Displays the Open Dialog Box.
Do Nothing	Launches Home Page without opening or displaying anything

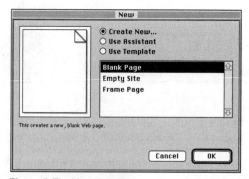

Figure 5. The New dialog box.

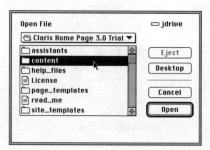

Figure 6. The Open dialog box.

APPENDIX A: APPLICATION PREFERENCES

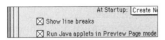

Figure 7. You must enable Java applets for them to run in preview mode.

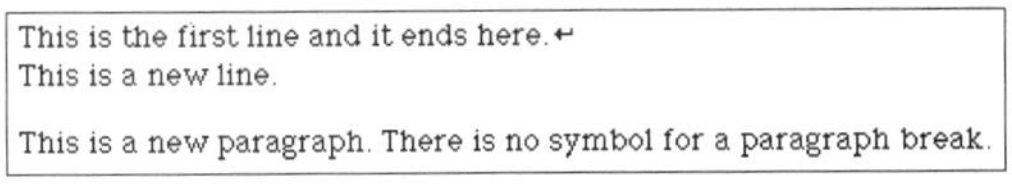

This is the first line and it ends here. ↵
This is a new line.

This is a new paragraph. There is no symbol for a paragraph break.

Figure 8. The line break character as it appears in a Home Page window.

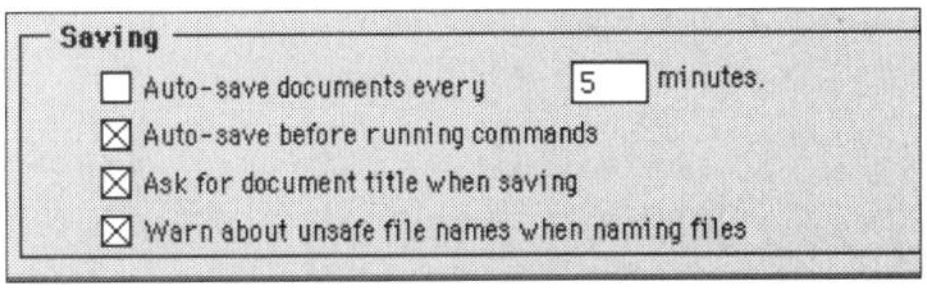

┌ **Saving** ───────────────────────
│ ☐ Auto-save documents every [5] minutes.
│ ☒ Auto-save before running commands
│ ☒ Ask for document title when saving
│ ☒ Warn about unsafe file names when naming files
└──────────────────────────────

Figure 9. The options in the Saving Section of the General tab.

Show line breaks

Selecting the Show line breaks check box (**Figure 7**) will insert a the bent arrow symbol representing a line break within a paragraph (**Figure 8**). Full carriage returns, which begin new paragraphs, have no symbol.

Run Java applets in Preview Page mode

This check box (**Figure 7**) controls whether Java applets can run while the document is in Preview Page mode. If the box is not checked, a placeholder will appear instead of the running applet, thus taking up less memory and making the application run faster.

Auto-save documents every _ minutes

This check box in the Saving section will make Home Page automatically save your work at a regular interval that you specify.

Auto-save before running commands

When this check box is selected, Home Page will save your work automatically before previewing, consolidating, verifying links, or uploading. If you uncheck this item, Home Page will still prompt you to save before running any of these commands.

Ask for document title when saving

Checking this box makes it so you have to have a title for your document when you save it, which avoids accidentally loading files called untitled.html.

Warn about unsafe file names when naming files

Selecting this check box makes Home Page display a warning screen when a file does not conform to standard HTML file naming conventions, and gives you the opportunity to change the file name. If you are planning on using HTML instead of HTM for your file extension, uncheck this box. Either one will work fine on any system.

✔ Tips

- If you're wondering what a preference does, run your cursor over it and look for the tips that display at the bottom of the Preferences window (**Figure 10**).

- It's a good idea to select the auto save, name prompt, and warning check boxes to give yourself an extra measure of safety when it comes to file management.

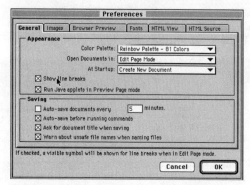

Figure 10. The text at the bottom of this window explains the functionality of the item your cursor points to.

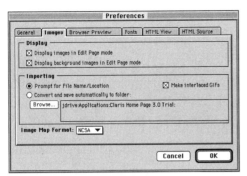

Figure 11. Displaying images can cause Home Page to run more slowly, so you can set the program to use a placeholder instead.

Figure 12. Uncheck these buttons to improve performance in Edit Page mode by not redrawing graphics.

Figure 13. Importing determines where converted graphic image files will be stored, and if these files should be interlaced in GIF format. You can either specify to be prompted for a file name and folder location, or have them automatically saved in a folder.

Figure 14. Click the Prompt for File Name/Location to see this dialog box each time Home Page converts an image to GIF format.

The Images Tab

The Images Tab has three sections: Display, Importing, and Image Map Format (**Figure** 11).

Display images in Edit page mode and
Display background images in Edit Page mode

Deselecting these Display check boxes (**Figure** 12) will speed up your computer's performance while you're working in Edit mode. Instead of showing your image, a placeholder with the name of the placed images appears on your page. You don't see anything telling you there's a background image set. Once you switch to Preview mode, both placed and background images are displayed.

Prompt for File Name/Location

When you select this radio button (**Figure** 13), Home Page will prompt you for a file name each time it converts a non-GIF/JPEG file into GIF format (**Figure 14**).

Convert and save automatically to folder

When you select this radio button, converted images are automatically named and saved to the folder you selected using the...

...Browse button

Use this button to designate the folder into which you want to automatically save converted GIF files.

Make interlaced GIFs

Select this check box if you want to automatically interlace converted GIF files.

Image Map Format (NCSA or CERN)

These settings are used for server-side image maps. If you are using one, ask your Internet Service Provider or system administrator which of these settings you should select.

APPENDIX A: APPLICATION PREFERENCES

159

The Browser Preview Tab

At this writing, two browsers dominate the marketplace: Microsoft's Internet Explorer and Netscape's Navigator. Use the Preview Browser One and Preview Browser Two Browse buttons to navigate to and select (**Figure 15**) the browsers you have installed on your system. These browsers are used to display your work in Preview in Browser mode.

The Fonts Tab

Home Page displays your HTML documents in the proportional and monospaced fonts you choose in the two windows of the Fonts tab (**Figure 16**). Select any font installed on your system by clicking the font list. Select point sizes from their size drop-down lists (**Figure 17**).

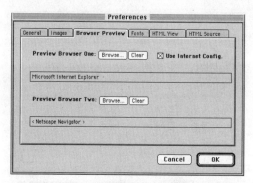

Figure 15. The Fonts tab, where you select fonts and point sizes for proportional and monospaced text while working in Home Page. These settings have nothing to do with how the text appears in a browser.

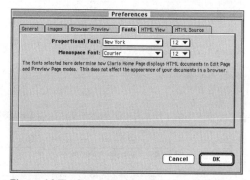

Figure 16. The Fonts tab, where you select fonts and point sizes for proportional and monospaced text in Home Page. These settings have nothing to do with how the text appears on your browser.

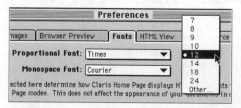

Figure 17. Select a point size from the drop-down list.

Use Defaults button

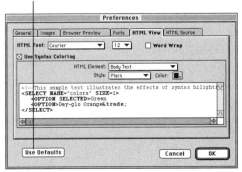

Figure 18. The HTML View tab controls the way code looks in Edit HTML Source mode.

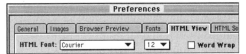

Figure 19. This is where you select the font to be used to display HTML code in Edit HTML Source mode, along with point size, and whether or not long lines of code are to be wrapped.

Figure 20. This check box controls Syntax Coloring, which shows different types of code in different colors.

Figure 21. To customize the appearance of code, select they type of code and choose a new style from the drop-down list or a color from the drop-down color palette.

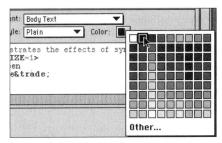

Figure 22. Each HTML element can display in a different color, which you choose from this palette.

The HTML View Tab

This tab is used to control how your page looks in Edit HTML Source mode (**Figure 18**).

HTML Font

Select the display font and point size for your HTML code using these drop-down lists (**Figure 19**). Checking Word Wrap will make all the longer lines of your code wrap to fit in your screen.

Use Syntax Coloring

When you select the Use Syntax Coloring check box, the drop-down lists in this window section control the colors of your HTML text (**Figure 20**).

You can assign each type of HTML code element a color and type style. To change an element color, select an HTML element and style from the drop-down lists (**Figure 21**), and a font color from the drop-down palette (**Figure 22**).

Each syntax type is represented in the preview window, and any change you make in color or type style will be instantly reflected there.

To return to the default settings for type style and color, click the Use Defaults button at the bottom of the HTML View tab window.

The HTML Source Tab

The settings in the HTML Source Tab (**Figure 23**) control the behavior of your HTML files.

Default HTML File Suffix

Every HTML file name must end with either .htm, or .html for it to function properly. This setting (**Figure 24**) designates which of these file extensions your HTML files will carry. If you are using a Windows NT server, you'll probably want to use "htm." Otherwise, "html" is a safe bet, especially if your server is either a Macintosh or UNIX system.

Header comment

This pop-up list (**Figure 25**) controls whether your pages will include an identification line at the top of the HTML code, as described in the table below. These comments won't display in browsers, but they can come in handy if you're trying to determine if your server hold the latest files.

Table 3. The Header comment pop-up list

LIST ITEM	WHAT IT DOES
Identify and time-stamp	Adds HTML line identifying application, date and time.
Identify as Claris Home Page file	Adds HTML line identifying application only.
None	No HTML identification line.

Line break format

These items control the invisible way your system represents line breaks. Macintosh systems use a Carriage Return (CR) character, UNIX systems use a Line Feed (LF) character, and Windows systems use both (CRLF). While this may be an issue if you're developing concurrently on different platforms, any of the selections will work perfectly in a browser, so best select the line break your system uses.

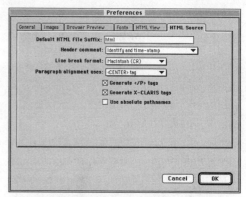

Figure 23. The HTML Source window controls behavior of HTML code produced by Home Page.

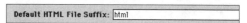

Figure 24. The file extension is entered in this window. Use HTM for NT servers, HTML for others.

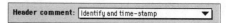

Figure 25. The Header comment window controls time stamping and identification of a file as being generated by Home Page. This setting has no effect on how a page is displayed in a browser.

Figure 26. You can choose to display the Claris information at the top of your HTML page, or not.

Figure 27. Paragraph alignment setting should be changed only if the browser you are using to test your pages is unable to center paragraphs of text.

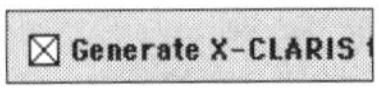

☒ Generate X-CLARIS

Figure 28. </P> tags are needed by older browsers. If you have trouble with displaying your pages, try clicking this check box to write "close paragraph" tags.

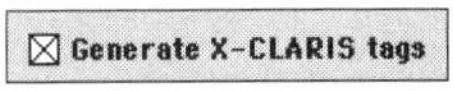

☒ Generate X-CLARIS tags

Figure 29. X-CLARIS tags are used by Home Page and do not effect the way a page looks in a browser.

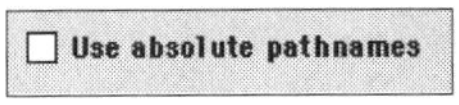

☐ Use absolute pathnames

Figure30. Absolute pathnames include information about the structure of your hard drive. Click this check box to use them. Relative file names need to be used when you upload your files to a server.

Paragraph alignment uses

There are two different ways to center text in HTML, using the <CENTER> tag or adding ALIGN=CENTER to another parameter, such as <P>. You probably won't need to worry bout this setting, but if you're ever testing your page in a browser and find that text isn't centering properly, try changing this setting in the Paragraph alignment uses drop-down list (**Figure 27**).

Generate </P> tags

In the early days of HTML, every <P> (which signifies the beginning of a new paragraph) had to have an ending </P> (signifying the end of a paragraph) to balance it out. This is no longer the case, but if there is any chance your page might be viewed with an old browser, check the Generate </P> tags check box (**Figure 28**) to have Home Page adhere to the old standard.

Generate X-CLARIS tags

Home Page uses several X-CLARIS tags not used or recognized by browsers to set up your page window. Selecting this check box (**Figure 29**) will include these additional tags in your HTML files. Your pages won't be affected by this, just the look of your HTML code will.

Use absolute pathnames

Select the check box (**Figure 30**) to reference the hypertext links that connect your files refer to their position on your hard drive (absolute) or their position relative to other files in your Web site (relative). If you select to use absolute file names, you will eventually have to gather your files into a folder and consolidate your image files before uploading your site to a server. The key to good file organization is to use a single folder for all your HTML files, and a nested subfolder for graphics and multimedia files.

APPENDIX B: SHORTCUTS

General Shortcuts

TO DO THIS	IN WINDOWS OS	IN MACINTOSH OS
Insert a horizontal rule	Click and drag the Insert Horizontal Rule button ▭ on the Basic toolbar to the position where you want to i insert the rule.	Click and drag the Insert Horizontal Rule button ▭ on the Basic toolbar to the position where you want to insert the rule.
Insert a table	Click and drag the Insert Table button ⊞ on the Basic toolbar to the position where you want to insert the table.	Click and drag the Insert Table button ⊞ onthe Basic toolbar to the position where you want to insert the table.
Move a window without bringing it to the front	Not available.	⌘-click on the window's title bar and then drag it.
Open an object editor for a form element	Right-click the form element (such as a check box or radio button) and choose *Form Object Editor* from the context menu.	Control - click the form element (such as a check box or radio button) and choose *Form Object Editor* from the context menu.
Open the Frame Object Editor	Right-click the frame and choose *Show Object Editor* from the context menu.	Control - click the frame and choose *Show Object Editor* from the context menu.
Switch to Edit HTML Source mode	Shift Ctrl H	Shift ⌘ H
Switch to Edit Page mode	Shift Ctrl E	Shift ⌘ E
Switch to Preview Page mode	Shift Ctrl P	Shift ⌘ P
Move the insertion point to the next or previous setting in a dialog box or object editor or to the next or previous cell in a table	Tab to move forward or Shift Tab to move back	Tab to move forward or Shift Tab to move back

Text Shortcuts

To do this	In Windows OS	In Macintosh OS
Select the next or previous paragraph	[Shift] [Ctrl] [↓] or [Shift] [Ctrl] [↑]	[Shift] [Option] [↓] or [Shift] [Option]-[↑]
Select text from the insertion point to the end or the beginning of the document	Not available.	[Shift] [⌘] [↓] or [Shift] [⌘] [↑]
Select a range of characters	[Shift] [→] or [Shift] [←]	[Shift] [→] or [Shift] [←]
Select a range of whole words	[Shift] [Ctrl] [→] or [Shift] [Ctrl] [←]	[Shift] [Option] [→] or [Shift] [Option] [←]
Delete the previous or following word	[Ctrl] [Backspace] or [Shift] [Delete]	[Option] [Delete] or [Option] [⌫]
Copy selected text	[Ctrl] - drag the text to the position where you want to place the copy.	[Option] - drag the text to the position where you want to place the copy.
Insert a non-breaking space	In Edit Page mode, press [Alt] and type 0160 on the numeric keypad.	[Option] [Spacebar]
Insert a line break.	[Shift] [Enter]	[Shift] [Return]
Create a new list item	[F8]	[⌘] [Return]
Create a new list item and indent it	Place the insertion point in the list and press [F9]	Place the insertion point in the list and press [Option] [⌘] [Return]
Create a new list item and indent it to the previous level of indentation (decrease indent)	Place the insertion point in the list and press [F7]	Place the insertion point in the list and press [Shift] [3] [Return]

Library Shortcuts

TO DO THIS	IN WINDOWS OS	IN MACINTOSH OS
Make a library entry using selected text	Drag the text to the left section of the library window.	Drag the text to the left section of the library window.
To perform various tasks on selected objects in the library window	Right-click the selected object and choose various options from the context menu.	Control - click the selected object and choose various options from the context menu.

Links Shortcuts

TO DO THIS	IN WINDOWS OS	IN MACINTOSH OS
Open the Link Editor	Ctrl L or Enter (numeric keypad) with Number Lock off.	⌘ L or Enter (numeric keypad) with Number Lock off.
Create a link	Select the text or image, right-click it, and choose *Link to File* from the context menu. You can also choose a file listed under *Link to Recent URL* or *Link to open file* in the context menu.	Select the text or image, Control-click it, and choose *Link to File* from the context menu. You can also choose a file listed under *Link to Recent URL* or *Link to open file* in the context menu.
Test a selected link in Edit Page mode	Right-click the link and choose *Follow Link* from the context menu.	Control - click the link and choose *Follow Link* from the context menu.
Remove a selected link	Right-click the link and choose *Remove Link* from the context menu.	Control - click the link and choose *Remove Link* from the context menu.
Insert an anchor in place of selected text	Right-click the selected text and choose Insert Anchor from the context menu. **Note:** Claris Home Page names the anchor for you.	Control - click the selected text and choose Insert Anchor from the context menu. **Note:** Claris Home Page names the anchor for you.
Insert a link to an anchor	Ctrl - drag the anchor to the location on the page or on another page where you want to create the link.	Option - drag the anchor to the location on the page or on another page where you want to create the link.

Images and Image Map Shortcuts

To do this	In Windows OS	In Macintosh OS
Return a selected image to its original size (width and height)	Double-click the lower-right corner handle of the image border.	Double-click the lower-right corner handle of the image border.
Return a selected image to its original width	Double-click the right handle of the image border.	Double-click the right handle of the image border.
Return a selected image to its original height	Double-click the bottom handle of the image border.	Double-click the bottom handle of the image border.
Resize a selected image proportionately	Hold down [Shift] and drag the lower-right corner handle.	Hold down [Shift] and drag the lower-right corner handle.
Replace a "missing image" icon with a new image	Right-click the icon, choose *Browse Files* from the context menu, and select the new image.	Control-click the icon, choose *Browse Files* from the context menu, and select the new image.
Open the Image Object Editor	Double-click the image or right-click the image and choose *Image Object Editor* from the context menu.	Double-click the image or [Control] - click the image and choose I*mage Object Editor* from the context menu.
Open an image in the Transparency and Interlacing Image Editor	[Ctrl] - double-click the image.	[Option] - double-click the image.
Open the Image Map Editor	Right-click the object and choose *Image Map Editor* from the context menu.	[Control] - click the object and choose *Image Map Editor* from the context menu.
Move a selected hot spot 1 pixel in the Image Map Editor	Press the arrow keys.	Press the arrow keys.
Move a selected hotspot 10 pixels in the Image Map Editor	Hold down [Ctrl] while pressing the arrow keys.	Hold down [Option] while pressing the arrow keys.
Resize a selected hotspot 1 pixel in the Image Map Editor	Hold down [Shift] while pressing the arrow keys.	Hold down [Shift] while pressing the arrow keys.
Resize a selected hotspot 10 pixels in the Image Map Editor	Hold down [Shift] [Ctrl] while pressing the arrow keys.	Hold down [Shift] [Option] while pressing the arrow keys.

Appendix C:

HTML Code Reference

While Home Page requires no knowledge of HTML, from time to time you may find it interesting to view the source code for the pages you're building in Edit HTML Source mode. Not only will this make you appreciate all the work Home Page does, it's a really good way to learn HTML.

One of the best references for learning HTML is another book in this series, *HTML for the World Wide Web: Visual QuickStart Guide*, by Elizabeth Castro. In the quickly evolving world of HTML, having a current reference at your side is something you should consider.

All pages of code follow the same syntax: They begin with <HTML> and end with </HTML>, and have any number of elements and tags in between. These are open and close paired tags, and many HTML commands follow this model. Some commands require only a single statement, such as <HR>, which inserts a horizontal rule.

Home Page adheres to the standards of HTML version 3.2 and several HTML extensions recognized by browsers.

Following is a list of all HTML tags.

Document-formatting Tags

TAG	WHAT IT DOES
\<HTML>...\</HTML>	HTML code between these markers
\<HEAD>...\</HEAD>	Defines head section of page
\<TITLE>...\<TITLE>	Defines title of page
\<DOCTYPE>	Defines the document's type
\<ISINDEX>	Enables searching
\<META>	Provides meta information about page
\<LINK>	Defines link relationship with another page
\<BASE>	States the location of the document
\<SCRIPT>...\</SCRIPT>	Defines an inline script
\<STYLE>...\</STYLE>	Defines style specifications.
\<MULTICOL>	Defines a multicolumn page layout
\<BODY>...\</BODY>	Defines the body section of a page
\<!—comment—>	Programmer's comments
\<!—NOEDIT>...\<!—/NOEDIT>	Defines an area to be left alone by Home Page

Text-Formatting Tags

TAG	WHAT IT DOES
<B>...</B>	Formats bold text
<I>...</I>	Formats italic text
<U>...</U>	Formats underlined text
<TT>...</TT>	Formats monospaced font text
<FONT>...</FONT>	Controls text font size and color
<BIG>...</BIG>	Increases point size of text
<SMALL>...</SMALL>	Decreases point size of text
^{...}	Displays text as superscript
_{...}	Displays text as subscript
<STRIKE>...</STRIKE>	Displays text as strike-though
<EM> ...</EM>	Displays emphasized text
<STRONG>...</STRONG>	Displays strong text
<DFN>...</DFN>	Displays text as a term's definition
<CODE>...</CODE>	Displays text as code
<SAM>...</SAM>	Displays text as a sample
<KBD>...</KBD>	Displays text as keyboard input
<VAR>...</VAR>	Displays text as a variable
<CITE>...</CITE>	Displays text as a citation
<BLINK>...</BLINK>	Blinks text
<MARQUEE>...</MARQUEE>	Displays text as a scroll across the window
<WBR>	Defines a hyphen to accommodate line breaks

Paragraph-Formatting Tags

TAG	WHAT IT DOES
\<P>...\</P>	Defines a paragraph
\ 	Inserts a line break inside a paragraph
\<NOBR>...\</NOBR>	Prevents line breaks in a paragraph
\<DIV>...\</DIV>	Aligns sections of a document
\<CENTER>...\</CENTER>	Centers elements in a document
\<PRE>...\</PRE>	Displays text in a monospaced font
\<BLOCKQUOTE>...\</BLOCKQUOTE>	Indents text as a quotation
\<ADDRESS>...\</ADDRESS>	Displays text as an address reference
\<UL>...\</UL>	Defines a bulleted list
\<OL>...\</OL>	Defines a numbered list
\<DIR>...\</DIR>	Defines a directory list
\<MENU>...\</MENU>	Defines a menu list
\<LI>...\</LI>	Defines a list item
\<DL>...\</DL>	Defines a definition list
\<DT>...\</DT>	Defines a definition term
\<DD>...\</DD>	Defines a definition
\<H6>...\</H6>	Defines text as the smallest (level 6) heading
\<H5>...\</H5>	Defines text as a larger (level 5) heading
\<H4>...\</H4>	Defines text as a larger (level 4) heading
\<H3>...\</H3>	Defines text as a larger (level 3) heading
\<H2>...\</H2>	Defines text as a larger (level 2) heading
\<H1>...\</H1>	Defines text as the largest (level 1) heading

Graphics and Multimedia Tags

TAG	WHAT IT DOES
\<IMG\>	Inserts an image
\<LOWSRC\>	Defines a low-resolution image which loads prior to a high-resolution version of the image
\<SPACER\>	Inserts a space which acts like a transparent GIF file
\<HR\>	Inserts a horizontal rule
\<EMBED\>	Inserts a multimedia object onto the page
\<NOEMBED\> be displayed	Specifies an alternate file to be loaded if a multimedia file cannot
\<APPLET\>...\</APPLET\>	Specifies a Java applet
\<PARAM\>	Specifies parameters for a Java applet
\<TEXTFLOW\>...\</TEXTFLOW\>	Specifies alternate text to display if a Java applet can't be executed.

Links Tags

TAG	WHAT IT DOES
<A>...</A>	Defines a hyperlink
<MAP>...</MAP>	Indicates a client-side image map
<AREA>	Defines a hotspot on an image map Tables
<Table>...</Table>	Defines the bounds of a table
<TR>...</TR>	Defines a table's row
<TD>...</TD>	Defines a table cell
<TH>...</TH>	Defines a table header cell
<CAPTION>...</CAPTION>	Defines a table caption Forms
<FORM>...</FORM>	Defines the bounds of a form
<INPUT>...</INPUT>	Identifies an input field or button
<TEXTAREA>...</TEXTAREA>	Identifies a text area field
<SELECT>...</SELECT>	Identifies a selection area
<OPTION>...</OPTION>	Defines selection list options Frames
<FRAMESET>...</FRAMESET>	Defines a frameset
<FRAME>...</FRAME>	Specifies a frame

APPENDIX D:

OBJECT AND LINK EDITORS

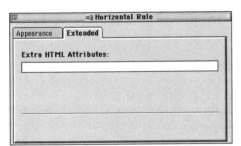

Figure 1. The Extra HTML Attributes field, accessible through the Extended tab in all Object Editor windows lets you manually add extra HTML tags to the selected object.

Object Editor button

Figure 2. One way to open an Object Editor is to select the object and click the Object Editor button on the Basic toolbar.

When you add objects to a page—tables, horizontal rules, frames, images, or hypertext links—you use an Object Editor or Link Editor to specify how each object appears and how it behaves.

Each Object Editor has at least two tabs, including one called *Extended* (**Figure 1**). The Extended tab offers an extra HTML Attributes field, where those with a taste for HTML programming can add extra HTML attributes to the selected object without having to switch to Edit HTML Source mode.

To open an Object Editor:

Select the object and click the Object Editor button on the toolbar (**Figure 2**).

or

Double-click the object.

or

Select the object and choose Object Editor from the View menu (Windows) or Show Object Editor from the Window menu (Mac).

The Horizontal Rule Object Editor

This Object Editor has just one main tab (Appearance) that controls just that, the look and placement of a horizontal rule (**Figure 3**).

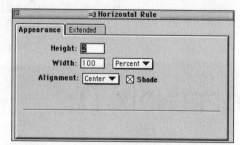

Figure 3. Control height, width, and shading of horizontal rules with this Object Editor.

The Horizontal Rule Object Editor: The Appearance tab

SETTING	WHAT IT DOES
Height	Controls the thickness of the rule, expressed in pixels. The default height is 2.
Width	Controls the width of the rule, either as a percentage of the browser window or as a fixed width expressed in pixels. The default width is 100 percent of the browser window.
Alignment	Controls horizontal rule alignment on a page. You may select to align the rule left, right, or center. The default setting is center.
Shade	If this check box is selected, the horizontal rule will have a 3-D, shadowed look. If deselected, the horizontal rule will be solid. The default setting is selected.

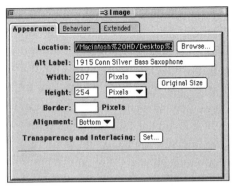

Figure 4. The Image Object Editor's Appearance tab gives you access to all the image attributes.

The Image Object Editor

The Image Object Editor has two main tabs: Appearance and Behavior.

The Appearance Tab

The Appearance tab has a number of settings that give you a lot of control over how your images look will look on the page (**Figure 4**).

The Image Object Editor: The Appearance tab

SETTING	WHAT IT DOES
Location	Contains the image file name and location. The location path always appears as an absolute reference to your hard drive.
Browse	Click this button if you want to change the image or if the Location field is empty, and use the dialog box to locate an image file.
Alt Label	Insert a descriptive name, which will be displayed if the image file does not load or if the receiving browser is set not to display images.
Width and Height	Controls image size (expressed in pixels or as a percentage of the browser window). To return the image to its original size, click Original Size.
Border	Adds a border to an image. Enter a value (in pixels). The default value is 0.
Transparency and Interlacing	Modifies a GIF image's transparency and interlacing options. Click the Set button to open the Transparency and Interlacing editor.

The Behavior Tab

The Image Object Editor's Behavior tab determines the function of the selected image (Figure 5).

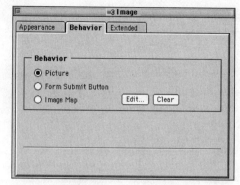

Figure 5. You can select only one of the radio buttons in the Image Object Editor's Behavior tab.

The Image Object Editor: The Behavior tab

SETTING	WHAT IT DOES
Picture	When this button is selected, the image will serve as just that, an image.
Form Submit Button	When this button is selected, the image will be used as a submit button in a form. When you select this option, enter *Submit* in the Alt Label field of the Appearance tab.
Image Map	When this button is selected, you can set designate hot spots on an image to use it as a client-side image map. Click the Edit button to open the Image Map Editor. To remove a hot spot from the image, click Clear.

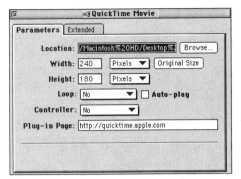

Figure 6. Use the Object Editor to set the properties of a QuickTime movie.

The QuickTime Object Editor

The QuickTime Movie Object Editor's Parameters tab controls the look and behavior of your QuickTime movies (**Figure 6**).

The QuickTime Object Editor

SETTING	WHAT IT DOES
Location	Displays the location of the selected QuickTime movie. If you want to change the movie, or if Home Page can't locate the selected movie, use the Browse button to locate a QuickTime movie.
Width and Height	Controls the dimensions of the movie. Note that the movie itself will not change size, just the border around it will. Width and height can be expressed in either pixels or as a percentage of the browser window. To return the dimensions to their original size, click Original Size.
Loop	Set this to No if you want the movie to stop after its first playing, Yes if you want the movie to loop continuously, or Auto-Reverse if you want the movie to loop alternately forward and backward.
Auto-play	Click this button to have the movie play automatically when a page opens.
Controller	Determines if the the movie controller (the scroll bar beneath the movie window) displays in the browser, so users can use to start and stop the movie.
Plug-in Page	If a visitor to your page does not have the plug-in required to view it, he or she will be directed to this Web address to download the plug-in.

The Link Editor

The Link Editor lets you set hyperlinks for selected objects (**Figures 7** and **8**). This window is expandable, with options to view URL syntax examples, Target Frame, and HTML options. It also lets you link to recent URLs and currently open files (**Figure 9**).

To open the Link Editor:

Select the object and click the Link Editor button on the Basic toolbar (**Figure 10**).

or

Select the object and choose Link to URL from the Insert menu.

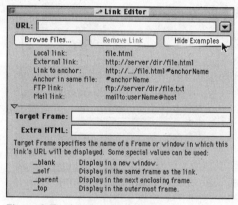

Figure 8. The fully extended Link Editor.

Figure 9. Click the triangle to the right of the URL field to access recently used URLs and open files.

Figure 7. The Link Editor in its simplest form.

Figure 10. The Link Editor button is one way to open the Link Editor.

The Link Editor

SETTING	WHAT IT DOES
URL	Contains the file name and path to the file to which you are linking. This link can be to a file on your hard drive, to an external link out on the Web, to an anchor anywhere on your site, or to an FTP server or e-mail address.
Last Files 🔽	Displays a list of both recent URLs and of all Home Page files currently open.
Browse Files	Lets you select a file on your hard drive.
Remove Link	Removes the link to a selected object.
Show/Hide Examples	Expands or contracts the top of Link Editor window to include or exclude URL syntax models.
Target Frame	Specifies the name of a requested frame or frame window on a linked page.

Anchor button

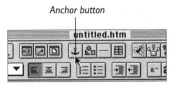

Figure 11. Click the Anchor button on the toolbar to create a anchor at the location of the insertion point, selected image, or text on your page.

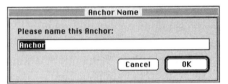

Figure 12. Make sure you choose distinct names for your anchors so that when you have multiple anchors on a page, they're easier to keep track of.

The Anchor Editor

Open the Anchor Editor by selecting an object or a text block, or by just placing the insertion point where you want to set an anchor location, then either clicking the Anchor button on the toolbar (**Figure 11**), or choosing Anchor from the Insert menu.

The Anchor Editor (**Figure 12**) has only one window, used to name the anchor. If you select a text block to be your anchor, this text will be the default name of the anchor. If you select an object or place an anchor next to text without highlighting the text, the anchor will be called *Anchor*. You can replace this default name with any name you choose.

The Table Object Editor

There are two tabs for this Object Editor
(**Figure 13**), Table and FileMaker. The latter is
used for making results tables in FileMaker
Pro links, an advanced procedure not covered
in this book.

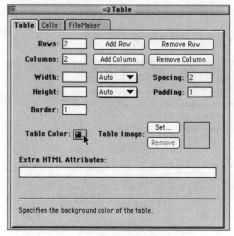

Figure 13. The Table Object Editor's Table tab
controls the physical attributes of an entire table.

The Table Object Editor: The Table tab

SETTING	WHAT IT DOES
Rows and Columns	Controls the number of rows and columns in a selected table. The default setting is two rows and two columns. Change the numerical values or click the Add and Remove buttons to adjust the number of rows and columns.
Width and Height	Controls table width and height, expressed either in pixels or as a percentage of the browser window, or set to automatically fit the size of cell contents.
Spacing	Controls the amount of space between cells.
Padding	Controls the amount of space around the cell's contents.
Border	Controls the thickness of the border around the table. Setting the border to zero makes the border invisible in the browser and in Preview Page mode: invisible borders appear as dotted lines in Edit Page mode.
Table Color	Click to open the color palette and assign a color as a table background.
Table Image	Click the Set button and locate the image file to use as a table background. Click Remove to remove the selected image.

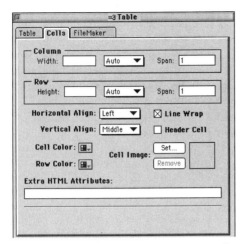

Figure 14. The Cells tab controls the attributes of individual table cells.

The Cells Tab

When you select a cell within a table, the Cells tab appears in the front of the Table Object Editor (**Figure 14**).

The Table Object Editor: The Cells tab

SETTING	WHAT IT DOES
Column and Row	Controls cell width and height, expressed either in pixels or as a percentage of the browser window, or set to automatically fit the size of cell contents.
Span	Combines a specific number of cells to span a row
Horizontal Align	Determines how elements in selected cells align horizontally: left, right or center.
Vertical Align	Determines how elements in selected cells align with respect to other cells: top, middle, bottom, or baseline.
Line Wrap	Select this check box to make text wrap within selected cells.
Header Cells	When checked, causes text within a selected cell to appear in boldface.
Cell Color	Use the drop-down palette to determine the background color of a selected cell.
Row Color	Use the drop-down palette to determine the background color of the row that includes the selected cell.
Cell Image	Sets an image as the background for a selected cell. Click the Set button to locate an image file. To remove an image, click Remove.

The Frame Object Editor

The Frame Object Editor controls frame-based page attributes.

The Contents Tab

The Contents tab assigns content and a name to a frame (**Figure 15**).

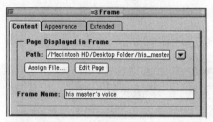

Figure 15. The Frame Editor's Contents tab.

The Frame Object Editor: The Contents tab

SETTING	WHAT IT DOES
Path	Enter the name of the page you want to fill the selected frame. Click the arrow to Link to a recent URL or link to an open file.
Assign File	Alternative method of assigning a frame page; click to locate a frame file.
Frame Name	Assign a descriptive name to the frame and enter it in this window.
Edit Page	Opens the selected file for editing (which cannot be done in a frame layout).

The Appearance Tab

The Appearance Tab controls how the selected frame looks in the frame layout (**Figure 16**).

Figure 16. The Frame Editor's Appearance tab.

The Frame Object Editor: The Appearance tab

SETTING	WHAT IT DOES
Size	Controls the size of the selected frame as a value expressed in pixels, a percentage of the browser window, or Stars, which takes all the remaining space.
Fixed Size	Select this check box if you don't want users to be able to resize the frame.
Margin Width and Height	Controls the distance content will be indented from the sides of the frame.
Scrollbars	Determines whether scrollbars will display in a frame window always, never, or only if they are needed to view the entire contents of a frame.
Show Border	When selected, the frame's border will be visible in the browser window.

Figure 17. The settings in the Form Object Editor must come from your systems administrator of Internet Service Provider.

The Form Object Editor

Double-click the Form Area's perimeter to open the Form Object Editor (**Figure** 17), which controls CGI script information.

The Form Object Editor

SETTING	WHAT IT DOES
Action	Insert the URL of the CGI script used to invoke a server-side forms handler here.
Method	Select Post or Get, depending on the specifications supplied by your systems administrator or Internet Service Provider.

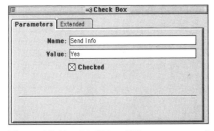

Figure 18. Use this Object Editor to name and set values for your check boxes.

The Check Box Object Editor

Double-click a check box within a Forms Area to open the Check Box Object Editor (**Figure** 18).

The Check Box Object Editor

SETTING	WHAT IT DOES
Name	Enter a descriptive name for the check box, for example "Send Catalog."
Value	Enter a value for the check box, for example "True."
Checked	When this option is selected, the box will be checked by default.

The Hidden Form Entry Object Editor

Hidden Form Entries send the server information needed to run a CGI script. They're only required by some CGI scripts and are not visible to the user. Use hidden fields only if your systems administrator or your Internet Service Provider instructs you to. Double-click the Hidden icon (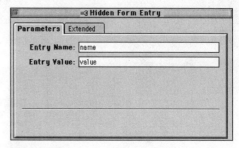) to open this Object Editor (**Figure 19**).

Figure 19. You'll only need to use this Object Editor for some CGi scripts as specified by your systems administrator or Internet Service Provider.

The Hidden Form Entry Object Editor

SETTING	WHAT IT DOES
Entry Name	Enter the name of the hidden entry, as requested by your systems administrator or your Internet Service Provider.
Entry Value	Enter the value of the hidden entry, as requested by your systems administrator or your Internet Service Provider.

The Password Field Object Editor

Double-click a Password Object you've placed in a Forms Area to open this Object Editor (Figure 20).

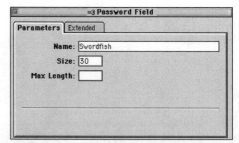

Figure 20. When text is typed in these fields, the characters display as asterisks or bullets.

The Password Field Object Editor

SETTING	WHAT IT DOES
Name	Enter the name assigned to the password field.
Size	Controls the width of the password field, expressed in characters.
Max Length	Controls the maximum number of characters that can be entered in a field.

APPENDIX D: OBJECT AND LINK EDITORS

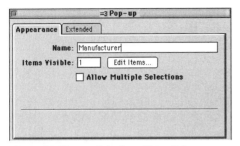

Figure 21. This simple looking Object Editor controls many complex pop-up menu functions.

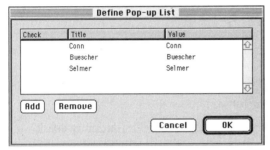

Figure 22. The Define Pop-up List window is where you'll do most of the work creating your list.

The Pop-up Object Editor

Pop-up menus and scrolling lists allow users to select from a list of items. The Appearance tab of the Pop-up Object Editor (**Figure 21**) determines form and function of pop-up menus and gives you access to the Define Pop-up List window (**Figure 22**).

A pop-up menu shows only one item in the list until the user clicks on it. A scrolling list shows more than one item, and users can scroll to see the remaining items in the list.

The Pop-up Object Editor

SETTING	WHAT IT DOES
Name	Assigns a name to the pop-up menu in the window.
Items Visible	Controls how many items display in the pop-up window.
Edit Items	Opens the Define Pop-up List window so you can assemble and edit the items in the pop-up list.
Allow Multiple Selections	Allows users to select more than one item from the pop-up list.

The Radio Button Object Editor

Radio buttons usually appear in sets, and only one of the buttons in the set can be selected. To open the Radio Button Object Editor (**Figure 23**), double-click a radio button you've placed in a Forms Area.

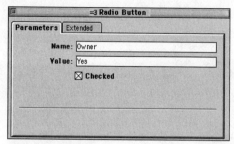

Figure 23. All button names should be the same but have different values as determined by the CGI script.

The Radio Button Object Editor

SETTING	WHAT IT DOES
Name	Controls the name assigned to a radio button.
Value	Controls the value for the button.
Checked	If this check box is selected, the radio button will be checked by default.

The Reset Button Object Editor

The Reset Button Object Editor has no settings, because this button does only one thing: reset the entries in the Forms Area (**Figure 24**).

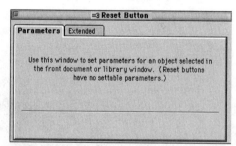

Figure 24. You won't be making changes in this Object Editor unless you want to use the Extended tab to add extra HTML attributes.

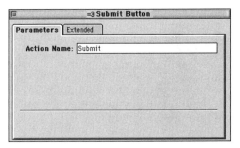

Figure 25. Unless specifically instructed otherwise, do not change the default name: *Submit.*

The Submit Button Object Editor

The Submit Button is Object Editor (**Figure 25**) is always be determined by the needs of your CGI script. This button lets users send the information they input to a form.

The Submit Button Object Editor

SETTING	WHAT IT DOES
Action Name	Specifies the name of the Submit button action. The requirements for this information come from your systems administrator or Internet Service Provider.

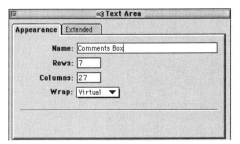

Figure 26. This Object Editor controls the size and behavior of the area users can enter text into.

The Text Area Object Editor

Open the Text Area Object Editor (**Figure 26**) by double-clicking a text area you've placed in your form area. Text areas let users enter lines of text, which they can scroll through using the scrollbars.

The Text Area Object Editor

SETTING	WHAT IT DOES
Name	Enter a descriptive name assigned to the text area.
Rows and Columns	Controls the number of rows and columns making up the text box.
Wrap	Controls the type of text wrap within the text area: Virtual, Physical, or none (Off).

The Text Field Object Editor

Double-click on a Text Field Object in a Forms Area to open the Text Field Object Editor (**Figure 27**). Text fields contain only one line of text (up to 500 characters long) and can be resized only horizontally.

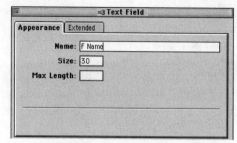

Figure 27. These fields are generally used for shorter information such as a name or phone number.

The Text Field Object Editor

SETTING	WHAT IT DOES
Name	Assigns a name to the text field.
Size	Controls the width of the field, expressed in characters.
Max Length	Controls the maximum number of characters that can be entered in the field.

INDEX

H

I

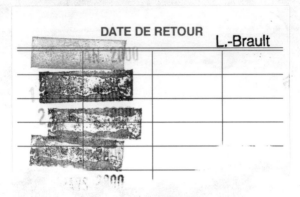

DATE DE RETOUR

L.-Brault